A Boy's Own Dale

*A 1950s childhood in the
Yorkshire Dales*

TERRY WILSON

EBURY
PRESS

1 3 5 7 9 10 8 6 4 2

Published in 2011 by Ebury Press, an imprint of Ebury Publishing
A Random House Group company
First published in the UK by Yorkshire Arts Circus in 1991

The Random House Group Limited Reg. No. 954009

Addresses for companies within the Random House Group can be found at
www.randomhouse.co.uk

A CIP catalogue record for this book is available from the British Library

The Random House Group Limited supports The Forest Stewardship Council
(FSC), the leading international forest certification organisation. All our titles that
are printed on Greenpeace approved FSC certified paper carry the FSC logo. Our
paper procurement policy can be found at www.rbooks.co.uk/environment

Printed in the UK by CPI Cox & Wyman, Reading, RG1 8EX

ISBN 9780091940218

To buy books by your favourite authors and register for offers visit
www.rbooks.co.uk

Contents

Part One

Part Two

Part Three

A
Boy's Own
Dale

Part One

TO

LONDON 236 MILES
Kirkby Lonsdale 17
HAWES   26
SKIPTON   16
LANCASTER 26

Grandad

✍

G randad was to do-it-yourself what a hammer is to brain surgery. So at seventy, when they made him retire from the gasworks, it seemed a bit strange for him to start working for Mr Frankland, who owned the sawmill and joinery works.

Fifty-odd years he'd worked at the gasworks as a stoker. The gasworks never stopped; all year round three men each had an eight-hour shift, and Grandad was one of them. If anyone was off the others had to cope.

When stripped to the waist Grandad's wiry, sinewy frame was a joke to the others. But many's the time I've seen the reflection of the white-hot retorts on the sweat of his body. He shovelled the coal into the open banks of retorts, working right

up to them with the long rake which he used to drag out the coke. The heat took your breath away.

Grandad never complained about his hands but they were nearly always bleeding from the deep cracks in them. They were worse in winter. Grandma used to get him small green blocks of Snowfire ointment to rub in. It stung like mad. I knew because I tried some once on a small cut. He never flinched.

Occasionally, on cold wintry nights, Gentlemen of the Road called in to lie on the bench for a warm. The men on the other shifts wouldn't stand for it, they sent the tramps packing, but Grandad didn't mind. He sometimes shared a sandwich with them. They didn't give him any trouble and I think it made him feel appreciated.

It was a long walk to the gasworks and Grandad always went over the field tops. The path was narrow, winding along the top of the meadows, a scary place at night, pitch black with just the far glow from the gasworks to guide you. I rarely went across there at night. For one thing, you couldn't see the cowclaps and

I always seemed to be unlucky. And even worse was the time when I jumped off the top of the stile right on to a group of cows lying down on the other side. I ran home as if Old Nick was behind me.

Once, when he'd just got back home from his night shift, Grandma was frying an egg for his breakfast and the kettle was boiling away. 'Just think Grandad,' I said, 'it's an important job, yours. Folks wouldn't be able to have eggs and brews if it wasn't for your gas, would they?' He gave me a perky little smile.

He was a proud man on Thursdays. It was pay day and he was the man of the house. My dad had died when I was very young so Mum and me lived with Grandad and Grandma. It was a ritual that Grandad always put his brown pay packet on the table. Then Grandma would open the cupboard where she kept her little treasures, like souvenir ashtrays from Morecambe and the Babycham glass that I pinched from the railway buffet. Out came the jars from the cupboard, the tops were unscrewed, the wage packet opened and the contents divided into little piles and put into the jars for different purposes, such as the penny policy death benefit from the union.

A brown ten-bob note was then given back to Grandad to last him the week. Grandad never said a word, never asked for more. He would smile, though, when he knew there was a bit extra and Grandma would say, 'Well done, lad.' Grandma's job was to get the best out of it. She never owed anybody anything. If she couldn't pay for it she didn't have it. Not till there was enough in the jar.

It was nice to watch this Thursday ritual and we always had Grandad's favourite for supper on pay day. Tatie hash – taties, meat, carrots and onions, all in a juicy gravy. It smelled lovely but Grandad couldn't tell because the gas had killed his sense of smell. 'It smells lovely today, Grandad,' I'd say and he'd nod approvingly. A drop of gravy often ran down a furrow to the bottom of his chin. 'Wipe your jib, Jakie,' Grandma would tell him. He'd smile and wink at me and mop up the gravy left on his plate with a crust from the loaf. Then he'd sit back in his chair and have a Woodbine followed by a good doze.

Mr Frankland's yard and mill were just at the back of our cottage. He also organised funerals, making coffins and doing all the arrangements. Grandma used to lay folks out for Mr Frankland when they died. He'd call round for her at any time, day or night. She cleaned the people up nice; whatever else they did was a secret but she used to get a pound for it. She knew what she was doing because she'd been in St John's Ambulance for years and had tons of medals to show for it.

Grandad liked his new job. He hadn't liked being retired for the two weeks it had lasted. His main job was to open and control the flow of water from the river through the sluice gate and into the dam which passed under the mill and ran the water wheel. It was another important job because, in effect, he controlled the whole business. A downpour in the hills, a flash flood and the wheels and leather belts went round like crazy in the joiner's shop to shouts of, 'Where's Jakie? Drop the sluice!'

He liked using the big circular saw underneath the mill. He had his own little kingdom down there and sawdust by the ton. It used to make me cringe, watching his fingers near that ripping wheel. He never had an accident, though, and his days passed happily.

The only problem at Mr Frankland's was in summertime. It was cricket. Grandma was a fanatic, especially since she could watch it on television. We got it in '53. She said it was for the Coronation but I had my suspicions. She watched every match, recording every ball on the back of an old envelope or Christmas card. She wanted Grandad to know exactly what had happened. As the sawmill was just outside our backyard he could pop in now and again to get the latest from the official scorer. The awkward bit was that Mr Frankland was equally keen and he did the same. It was funny to see them in our house, both sat on the same sofa when they should have been working; Mr Frankland suddenly didn't recognise Grandad and Grandad didn't recognise him.

Gilbert Aughton was another cricket fanatic. He watched every cricket match played in our village. He was their mascot. He and Grandad had been in the Duke of Wellington's Regiment during the Great War. They'd fought together all over France. It was something Grandad was really proud of. They were the only two old Dukes left in our area, and every time they met, the friendly banter started. Grandad would say, 'I see you've not been in Lambert's window yet.' That's the newspaper shop where little cards go in the window to tell you you're dead. Gilbert would say, 'Well I'm okay so long as him up there keeps putting on the slow bowlers. I just have to watch out for the odd googlie!' Gilbert died before Grandad. 'He's put me in as last bat,' said Grandad sadly.

Grandad's bonus at the mill came whenever he was asked to help Cyril Kershaw, the craftsman joiner. It happened twice a year when batches of coffins were made for stock. Loved helping to make coffins did Grandad. He polished the wood till you could see your face in it. It was a funny chain of events when you think about it. Someone would die, Mr Frankland would come for Grandma to do the laying out and Grandad would say, 'I've got the perfect fit.'

One winter Cyril decided his days were getting numbered. Just like a Pharaoh he decided to construct his own masterpiece from the thickest, finest oak; totally draughtproof. Dinnertime and any other free time, Cyril spent on his coffin. He kept it in a special corner, covered with a cloth. But Cyril lived longer than he'd reckoned and the coffin got more and more ornate with beautiful carvings all round it. This didn't please Grandad because it was the one coffin he'd not let Grandad help with, not let him even touch.

Cyril left it out one dinnertime while he did an errand so Grandad took the opportunity and tried it for size. It was a sunny day, he nodded off and someone put the lid on. Cyril came back and started chipping away at the side of the coffin. It's a wonder poor old Cyril didn't take occupancy there and then with the shock it gave him. They say the doctor came quick enough – but Cyril never talked to Grandad again!

When Grandad got into his eighties he couldn't do as much as before so then he got his third job. Mr Frankland put him in charge of the yard at the back of our cottage where deliveries were made. Grandad put up a sign saying, DRIVERS REPORT TO JAKIE'S. It gave him an interest until he retired permanently.

Every day he walked Chippy, his old brown dog, over the river bridge, down the riverside fields and round by the gasworks. They'd stopped making gas by then but he walked round the site and back over the field tops. On a bad day, the walks got shorter and the dog walked badly too. On a good day Grandad would whistle and the dog was like a young 'un again.

Two years before Grandad died, the new doctor, Jim Bentley, was going through patients' record cards. He'd just thrown one out belonging to a woman who'd have been a hundred and twenty years old if she'd still been alive. Then he came across one for Francis Jacob Heard. 'And he'd have been nearly a hundred,' the doctor told his nurse, 'and no record of ever being ill.' Just as he was starting to tear it in half she said, 'You'd better not do that. It's old Jakie's – and he's just gone past the window with his dog.'

'I think he's about due for a visit then!' decided the doctor.

In Grandad's young days, doctors cost money and nature's home remedies were always the order of the day. Nevertheless, he enjoyed Dr Jim popping in during his last years to see that he was all right.

He was still first up in the morning, clearing the ashes and lighting the fire. And he never let me use my alarm clock; he liked to give me my seven o'clock call to get me up for work. I was never late.

Eventually he had a stroke. Dr Jim said he'd only last a few days and that he could arrange to have him taken into hospital. We wanted him to die at home and Dr Jim agreed that would be best.

The afternoon he passed away his family and dog were beside him. Dr Jim came and so did Mr Frankland but it wasn't a sad affair. Mr Frankland brought him the finest coffin I'd ever seen – it was beautiful. We all sat round, having a cup of tea and reminiscing about the old lad.

'Where's Grandad's teeth?' Mr Frankland asked at one point.

'They're in his waistcoat pocket where they've been for the last ten years,' I told him. We all decided they should be put in the coffin for the afterlife to give him a good start. 'Shall we put the axe in as well?' somebody said. 'He loved chopping firewood!'

The dog stayed by the coffin all night.

Mr Frankland brought the hearse. He then did something unusual. Folk couldn't remember him having done it before in the thirty years he'd been in business. With his bowler on, he walked in front of the hearse the mile and a half to the churchyard. Something else was also strange. God seemed to have stopped all the traffic. There were no cars at all on that road but us.

I put a little message into the coffin with him, on the back of a photo of him taken in the trenches in France – 'A trooper till the last.'

Starting School

〜

I learned the difference between boys and girls at the age of five. The girls and us infants had the front playground. The boys had the back one. There were no young boys down our street and I'd been quite happy playing in the meadows with Brenda Preston, but now they were forcing all this on me.

Starting school did not appeal. What's more I couldn't pronounce my Rs. 'Wun Wabbit Wun,' I puffed on regular escapes to the fields and river. Even a year or two later when asked what I'd been doing at school that day, the reply, 'Weeding,' brought some astonished looks and a 'Good God!' from Grandad. Hopes, rather than expectations, followed my progress.

The school sheltered under the hillside, by the side of Cragdale Rock, which is an imposing cliff with a pole on the top and a flag for important days. Cragdale Rock juts out like a face over the market place, watching all that happens in the little town.

So there I was on my first day, destined for Mrs Bell's infant class, going up the steep narrow lane of School Hill with Grandad leading. Lots of kids I didn't know, all ages and sizes, were also climbing that hill, swinging pump bags and chattering. I felt for my hankie and put it back. Instead I clutched tighter on my bag of yellow kali that Grandad had got me from Betty Bilton's sweet shop as we'd passed.

Mrs Bell was at the school gate and the yard was surrounded by iron railings with spikes on the top. They'd make good spears, I thought. It looked like a prison. Grandad disappeared back down the hill into the mist. He didn't come in with me, he was too busy at the gasworks, he said. And I could have been busy down the river.

In Mrs Bell's classroom there were pegs for hats and coats. I decided I'd keep my hat and coat on, save me from having to keep watching that peg. Anyway I wasn't stopping for long. I think Mrs Bell understood, she said she'd keep a good eye on me. That was nice.

Toys were everywhere. And a sandpit, but not the sort of sand you get by the river. I said I could show them where the proper stuff was if they wanted. Mrs Bell smiled and pointed to a wooden rocking horse. I tugged at her dress and told her that Doris, Tommy's carthorse, was having her shoes changed that morning if she'd like to come and see. She walked over to a toffee jar, unscrewed the top and started giving everyone a sweet. I pushed my kali deeper into my pocket. It was a strange-looking sweet, like a tiny egg only yellow and squeezy. I bit and it spurted. Fishy! It was horrible. Good job I'd got the kali. I had a quick dip but she was coming round again so I shoved the kali back in my pocket and waited with eyes like a cornered rabbit. This time it was a big brown jar with the picture of a sun on it. She put a spoon in, twirled it round and brought it out. Brown treacly-looking stuff. But I wasn't poorly and I didn't want to be!

'You'll like this,' she said persuasively, 'it's malt.'

'I'm expecting Grandad any minute,' I tried to protest as the spoon found its mark. 'That's nice,' I relented, licking my lips, 'I'll have one of those tomorrow and save the fishy one for Grandad. He'll like it.'

⁓

And so the summer days rolled on. Grandad was always there by the gate at home time. Now and again Doris the carthorse and Tommy passed us. She knew me and would stop so we'd get on the back.

Mrs Bell liked taking us for walks on summer afternoons. A crocodile, in twos, holding hands, we'd go down Watery Lane. She showed us the watercress swaying in the clean water and let us take a bit but not too much. It tasted sharp. We munched it as we walked to the end of the lane, through the gate and up past the wood on the hillside. She told us we couldn't go in there because that's where the reservoir was, providing all the water for our homes. I wondered how it got to our house and whether Grandad knew it was there.

The hillside was covered in wild pansies and tiny strawberries. Lodge Pond was surrounded by bracken and teemed with all sorts of crea-  tures. It was heaven up there. Rabbits pricked up their ears and popped down their holes as they heard us approach. I'd never seen frogspawn before. Mrs Bell told us we needed a jam jar with some string for a handle. Then we could all have a little to take home and watch it grow into tadpoles. We also saw a toad up there, jumping around in the wet, spiky grass, but we couldn't catch it.

In autumn she showed us the berries, the seeds and the sycamore wings twisting down, the wonderful colours of the leaves, their shapes and the rustling. We kicked them up in a shower of gold.

The first flakes of snow meant balaclavas and mufflers. Mrs Bell taught us to look closely. All the flakes were different; all were perfection. There was time for only a fleeting glance before they turned to water on our hands. There were tracks in the fresh snow down by Watery Lane. How would the creatures that lived there survive, I wondered?

As winter set in, she told us stories and we'd sit round her and listen. Then when it came to Christmas we heard sleigh bells in the school-yard. We had a visitor – Santa knew Mrs Bell. It was magic.

When spring came I had to move up a class and it wasn't the same. We never went outside except at playtime and there were no more visits to Watery Lane. Mrs Morley's class was different. Instead of sitting in a circle, we all sat at desks in rows. I had to do things I didn't understand – read words from books and get them right. 'I have a small house. It's not bad for me, I'm only a mouse.' And a picture. The stories were silly. Mice don't live in houses.

Eventually the time came to leave the infants' classes; move up again, change playgrounds. More new teachers, new things to do, new things to learn. There were four classrooms with a hall in the middle and peeling paint everywhere.

We were all together for prayers in the morning. Mrs Pickles on the piano played 'All things bright

and beautiful, all creatures great and small ...'
Mr Pickles was in charge. He just looked on.
There were large windows which needed cords to
open the top part; on a bright day the sun poured
in through them.

Lots of things happened in the hall. Most
important was dinner. Donnie Thwaites brought
the dinner in his van, in shiny big drums with
tops that snapped tight. We lined up with our
plates. A 'please' and 'thank you' brought more
than a smile from the white-pinnied dinner
ladies, especially when it was prunes. I got lots of
those. Tinker, tailor, soldier, sailor, richman,
poorman, beggarman, thief. Stones lined up
round the edge of the plate kept slipping back
into the custard.

Winter milk was not good as it always froze
and the cardboard tops rose up. The milk bottles
were put on the pipes to thaw and then it tasted
horrid. I collected the tops and used them to
make pompoms with scraps of wool. It was good
fun on winter nights.

Our band played in the hall. Mrs Pickles called
it percussion and I think she enjoyed it more

than anybody. We had a blackboard with large sheets of music on it. The dots meant nothing to me. I never got past triangle, never a cymbal, never a drum. How can you play high or low on a triangle?

When we were singing she'd ask, 'Who's grunting?' I played it safe and just mouthed the words. What I hated most was country dancing when we had to skip around with girls. 'Be happy,' Mrs Pickles would cry.

Christmas was a special time in the hall – if you could recognise your own jelly. We'd have a Jacob's Join. Everyone took something; mince pies, jellies, blancmanges, and they were shared out with a, 'Watch out for that yellow jelly – it's smelly so and so's.'

There were a few things I didn't enjoy in that hall, such as the School Doctor's visit. The doctor was a lady – a rough lady. We'd line up and she'd look at our ears and search through our hair looking for nits. It wasn't nice. The very worst of all, though, was the dentist. We lined up and went into his van in turn. He never talked and it always hurt. He put a brace on my teeth with horrible wires and things. Some kids laughed at me.

The hall in spring had a wonderful smell. Three bulbs to a bowl and the blue hyacinths smelled strongest. I'd stay there at playtimes and walk round the bulbs. Mrs Pickles noticed so I got a special job, helping her with the bulb planting every autumn. We took bowl after bowl up into the attic of the school house. In spring we brought them back down and I proudly set them on the window ledges, where they watched me try to learn. I watched them too, but there always

seemed to be more happening the other side of the glass.

At the bottom end of the hall was a big board with drawing pins in. The first time I saw it there was nothing on it, only a cardboard sign at the top saying Current Affairs. It puzzled me. I knew of currant buns and currents in the river; they were good. But 'Affairs aren't nice things,' Grandma told me when I asked. So I decided I'd have nothing to do with Current Affairs.

I concentrated on the nature table halfway along the side of the hall. Now that was interesting. There were carrot tops growing in saucers, beans in a jar of wet cotton wool, ants in white plaster with tunnels and a glass front and newts in an empty fish tank with stones. But strangest of all was a moleskin – so soft. I'd never felt one before and I wondered how he kept it so clean in all that soil. In the autumn the nature table was a picture. We all collected berries and seeds, put them on cardboard and wrote on it what they were. I did best at that, better than at lessons. I knew well the woodlands, the crags and the moors. Sometimes they'd wonder at the things I had on my card but I kept it secret where I found them. I was often alone but never lonely out in the countryside, not with the wildlife, the plants and the birds.

We got points at school for all sorts of things, not just lessons. A bag of cherries would get you a kiss from the teacher too. I used to borrow Grandad's shears and tidy the lawn by the school house. It earned the same number of points but no sloppy kiss.

The same thing happened with flowers. The well-to-do brought fancy ones wrapped up posh from shops, some I'd never seen before. I struggled up School Hill with armfuls of proper flowers from meadows and woods, a few from here, a few from there. And just once a year, I brought a few wild orchids. I walked miles to that special spot and if there weren't many I'd leave them. We made all the flowers up into vases. Then at play-time I rearranged the vases on the window ledges so mine got the best sun.

⌒

It wasn't easy to hold your own in education but I was important in lessons when I got my new job. I was in charge of the books, putting them out and taking them back, while the others had playtime. I didn't mind, and it was often safer inside.

It was one of those times that I saw it at the back of the bookcase. *Just William* it was called. I flicked a few pages. William and Henry got up to all sorts. It was a new story every chapter. I'd never liked books, not since that mouse and his silly little house, but this was interesting. From then on I'd charge round the desks, launch the

books back into the case, get *William* out and sit on the pipes in the corner behind the blackboard. My eyes rolled with the pages till one day Mrs Pickles saw me and I hurriedly put it back.

The children came in from playtime; it had been snowing and

I hadn't even noticed. 'We're going to have a story now,' said Mrs Pickles. 'Terry will tell you one about William and Henry. Stand at the front, Terry.'

I wobbled to my feet and started. 'Well I've just been reading about the time that William went round to Henry's ...' And I told them the story as well as I could remember it and sat down.

Mrs Pickles clapped and everyone nodded. And that's how it went on. Whenever she was called away, I was asked up to tell another story. I liked it and I took time preparing my 'lessons'. I never wanted it to end but the book, sadly, did. I didn't tell anybody, though. I stood in front of the class, making stories up as I went along. Each day Grandma always asked me what I'd done in school. I'd tell her, 'We had sums, the times table up to nine, prunes for dinner and two lots of William!' Everybody liked my stories and I really felt I was somebody, not just the book minotaur. The dictionary said 'a bull with one horn'. I never puzzled that one out.

§

It seemed no time at all before we had to move up again. Mr Pickles had the top class but he didn't need my stories, other things were more important. There was a big brown wireless we were often made to listen to.

One particular day, as snowflakes fell and a bluetit chipped at the new putty on the windows, the wireless crackled out about cocoa and where it came from. I knew ours came from the Co-op. Our number was 733 and we got Divi on it. Now apparently this cocoa stuff was grown in Brazil, they brought it to England on boats, made chocolate from it and sold it to Betty Bilton's sweet shop at the bottom of School Hill. Well, I never! I soon decided I'd better tell Grandad. He was good with spuds so we'd save a fortune.

Mr Pickles switched the wireless off when the programme ended. 'Mr Bournville is having a competition,' he said. 'We must all write a story about a cocoa bean because all the schools are entering.'

Grandma bought me my first Biro. No messy nibs or inkwells for me. I didn't want a smudge or a spidery blob as I told Mr Bournville all about Betty Bilton and how important she was.

Some time afterwards the school got a parcel. Mr Pickles called everyone together into the hall – and me to the front. 'William and Ethel were …' I began. He stopped me and smiled, then read out a letter written in coloured, posh writing from Mr Bournville. It mentioned my name and said I'd won the competition. Mr Pickles shook my small hand and gave me the letter. And the parcel. Ten bars of chocolate. No Betty for a whole week. And I had lots of friends.

∽

One morning things were suddenly very different in the big hall; they'd put desks in there. We'd soon have to go, we were told. I didn't understand, didn't they want us any more? The Eleven Plus they said it was, and how well we did would decide which school we'd go to next. We were given papers with lots of questions. Where would I go? Who's got some *William* books? Mr Pickles said, 'Shush.' The bluetit pecked at the putty again. He had a friend with him this time.

Tommy and Doris

〜

From the front door of our cottage you could see the fells all the way back to Attermire and Highfell. To the back was the meadow, the stream at the far side, the marsh marigolds and kingcups.

It was where Doris the carthorse played. In the summer she lived there when she'd done her daily work. Tommy, who looked after her, always wore braces and a thick leather belt. He would lead her to the gate and let her loose. She'd gallop with the force of an army, then throw herself on to her back, legs kicking.

'Again, Doris, again!' us kids shouted. She usually did it again, then came over to where we were sitting on the wall. She'd nudge us with her big face, we'd pat her and give her a crust, then she'd be off again.

We liked going to Tommy's stable at the end of the cottages. It was a wonderful smell when the smoke came up as he shoed Doris. We winced a bit in case it hurt but Tommy said it didn't. Then he used to share out the old nails between us but best of all was if we got one of her shoes.

As summer rolled on Tommy would fence off the bottom part of the meadow to provide hay for Doris in the winter. When the men were done scything it, we were let in to rake the grass into rows, singing and laughing and bouncing about. This was our passport to ride on Doris's cart for the next year.

A tin poster was nailed to the wall in her stable. It was an advert for Guinness, showing a man holding a carthorse above his head on one arm. Tommy said it was him and Doris. He never did that trick for us, said he was always frightened of dropping her.

Tommy and Doris faded from this life together. I went into the stable some time later and the harness, brasses, old nails and shoes were still there. And a darkness I'd never known. I looked at the rusty Guinness poster.

Then I pinched it – to keep it safe.

To be a Fisherman

⌇

As a young lad, the river fascinated me. Clear and sparkling, tumbling away over the rocks, or fast and furious in a peaty spate. There was always something to do; walking around rock pools, exploring under every ledge and stone between the weir and the river bridge, chasing minnows, standing behind the waterfall. Hot, long summer days. That's when I'd see the fishermen come down to the river. Fly-fishermen casting lines of silent silk landing like thistledown, sucking trout making rings on the surface which rippled outwards. They talked amongst themselves, I was only a lad, I had to go home, but one day I'd be older and I'd be a real fisherman. I'd have a rod. I'd be a shadow at dusk

catching trout. Just dreams; reality was a long way off. First I'd have to learn to fly-fish. But I knew where the trout were. Every run, every trickle, every mood. I watched some nights from the bridge when the fishermen thought I'd gone. Some were good, some hadn't a clue. One day I'd show them where the real trout lurked.

It was fun and furtive tickling trout. It could only be done on summer days standing knee deep in the pools or laid on the rocks, leaning over the edges. I had to pretend it was only minnows and bullheads I was after, the trout were for the fishermen. The odd one was quickly slipped inside my shirt, then a fast scurry home, but mostly I let them go.

I could play with them, stroking them under the belly. Then they rolled over like a dog asking for more. They were my friends, my company. I did want to match wits with them, though. Often I would see no one all day but I was never lonely.

It seemed there were two problems. The first was a half-crown. I'd had one last Christmas in my stocking and without another one I'd be in bother.

Grandma was sat in the deckchair in the front garden, near the dark red peonies. She always had an odd coin in the back of her purse. I didn't want to bother her but I wanted to be a fisherman and she understood that half-a-crown for a licence was vital.

I watched Sid Clark at the ironmonger's fill in my name and address on the yellow licence. He kept peering down at me over the counter, muttering. As he gave it to me, I had a last look at the only two and sixpence I'd see between now and next Christmas, and handed it over. I was a fisherman. It was official, the licence said so.

Now to tackle problem number two, I thought, as I looked at the rods, reels and lines in the window. We had some long canes at home for the sweet peas. We had bobbins for sewing. We had string – green like the fly-fisherman's line. We had wire so I could make rings for the rod. I'd saved bits of nylon and a few rusty hooks found in the bushes by the river and an odd float too. I could also make flies from Uncle Tom's hen feathers.

It was a proud moment when at last I stood by my favourite pool. The challenge was on as I flicked the float under the bushes where the current runs in. It was a lovely evening and I was at peace with the world.

'What do you think you're up to?' It made me jump. I turned to face a fat, ruddy-faced man, wearing one of those hats that go forwards and backwards, full of fishing flies.

'Fishing, mister.' I told him.

'You need a licence to fish.'

I proudly reached inside my jerkin pocket and pulled it out. 'That's me, Terry Wilson.'

'I know who you are. You're always hanging about t'river. Now clear off.'

'But mister, I've got a licence.'

'Doesn't matter. You've not got permission so you can't fish here.'

'But it cost me half-a-crown, mister. Where can I fish then, please?'

'Nowhere. It's all ours. Haythorne Angling Club.'

'All of it?'

'Aye, all of it. Six miles upstream and six miles down. Now clear off.'

It was sad walking back home over the bridge. Three fellows made a joke about my tackle as I went round the corner. I didn't understand how the river could be all theirs. Surely not all of it. There was a club, I knew that. Mr Catlow, who ran the picture house, was in charge. He was nice. But all the members I saw fishing seemed well-off, beyond the hope of lads like me. Even if I had the money they'd not let me join. They kept it posh. It was a problem I hadn't bargained on. But was it all hopeless?

Saturday nights Grandma and Mrs Fell always went to the pictures, end seats in the bottom half. Would she ask Mr Catlow about it for me?

'Here you are, Terry,' she said as she came in from the pictures. 'Mr Catlow has sent you last year's rule book and it says they've had all that fishing stretch for years. It gives the names of all the members and there's a big waiting list to get in, mostly business people. Even then it costs five pounds to join. I'm sorry, love.'

I took the yellow book upstairs. A folding map fell out. It showed all the river from Stainforth to Wigglesworth. All the fishing rights the club owned were marked in black. I pored over it. It was nearly all black – but wait! There seemed to be the odd small gap.

I was about to invent the Terry Wilson fishing club, membership restricted to one. But there were a few people I'd got to go and see first.

Mr Frankland's sawmill was located between the weir and river bridge. It bordered the river with about three feet of grassy bank but there

was no way down to it. It was one of the banks on the fishing club map. Grandma laid out dead folks for Mr Frankland, so that had to be a point in my favour.

I found Mr Frankland in his timber yard. He listened to me and smiled sympathetically. 'So long as you promise not to fish it in a flood I might be able to help. Follow me.' We went under the shed with the green corrugated roof where the ladders were kept. 'Look over this wall,' he said. And there below was the river, eight or ten feet down. He picked up what looked like a coiled-up rope ladder but it was made of metal and wire. It was hooked on to the wall. 'We sometimes have to get down to the river to wash the buckets out,' he explained, 'so just toss the coil up over the wall and climb down, then bring it up when you've done. And a spare trout would do nicely, Terry, if you get one sometime.'

'Thanks ever so, Mr Frankland,' I called as I skipped away. Off to the next blank on the map – Lizzie Cox's!

Lizzie had the end cottage of six just below Mr Frankland's mill. Same thing there, a steep drop down to the river, but more importantly it was the last cottage before the bridge. The mill race went under all the cottage gardens and came out underneath hers. Now Lizzie sold sweets, pop and cigs from her back room. It was time to point out to Mrs Cox that I was probably her best customer!

I came out of her shop with a bag of mixed sherbet, a big smile on my face and a key for her back gate that I had to keep safe.

Home again and a good day's work done. It was time to mark up my map. I smiled as I went to sleep. Tomorrow would be Widdup's Paper Mill, a mile further along. It had a twenty-foot drop down to the river. But so what? They had windows, mostly broken, and I only needed one. It was a big, draughty place. Mum worked there and I helped her when I'd nothing to do.

By ten o'clock next morning I had promised Mr Widdup my undying loyalty. I'd agreed to pull his paper trucks across the yard on Saturday mornings in exchange for a window. Another mark on my map.

Next on the list, Jimmy Dodd's car dump behind his garage. It bordered the river. Rusting

junk everywhere but marvellous for finding ball bearings to use as marbles and Castrol oil drums for rafts. Now Jimmy liked to beat the system, so having explained I was up against a monopoly I soon added another mark to my map.

And so it went on. Dot after dot went on to my map and eventually the plan went into action. I started fishing.

'What the blazes is that?' said the two old blokes looking downstream from the top of the river bridge, as a sparkling twelve-inch trout was pulled along the surface by a little red float before disappearing under the bridge and heading for Lizzie Cox's. An astonished fly-fisherman from below the bridge looked on in disbelief. The two old blokes scurried across the road to see me hauling the fish up and over Lizzie's back wall. All legal just as long as I stood on my own patch. I had a dip of kali.

I started to become very unpopular with the fishermen. In fact, I was mystifying to some of them. Especially on the evenings when I walked home with two or three lovely trout. Conversations such as, 'Fishing's no good tonight – too clear,' suddenly stopped as I walked past. There were all sorts of questions. 'What's he carrying that cow's horn for? What's in it?' I wasn't telling, but I'd often watched trout nose stones to catch mayfly larvae. My horn was full of them.

Mayhem lasted all through the season as fish were spirited up to heaven through a window of Widdup's Mill and I regularly carried home big trout. Then one January evening Mr Catlow from the fishing club called at our house. 'Terry, we've just had our Annual General Meeting. They've

asked me to invite you to join our club. And no fee till you leave school, provided you follow our rules and only fish on our water.'

'Thank you, Mr Catlow.'

'Thank you, Terry,' he said winking. 'The Committee will be very relieved.'

Short Back and Sides

⁓

'Short back and sides, please.' I was never quite sure what it meant but that's what I was told to ask for every time.

I looked up at the sign saying JACK SAUNDERS BARBER. The bell jangled as I entered, passed by the counter and went around the glass partition. Four old chairs were lined up for waiting customers. I'd sit in the one near the wall, next to Denis Compton, Brylcreemed to perfection.

Mr Saunders also did shaves, stropping his cut-throat razor to get a sharp edge on it. I always thought of him as a responsible kind of man because he had this clock with a sign on it saying Surgical Rubberware, ready for any unexpected accident, I supposed. He was also very thoughtful.

As his customers paid up and were about to leave he always asked if they'd like anything for the weekend. If they nodded, he'd reach under the counter, put a small packet in a brown bag and pass it over.

I tried it once after my short back and sides. I asked him if I could have something for the weekend. He looked at my short pants, reached down under the counter and passed me a small brown bag.

It explained why he was always so discreet when I saw what was inside. I could understand grown men being too embarrassed to ask for sherbet lollies.

A Pair of Purdeys

❧

I'd decided I'd go and ask, see if it was true about
the beatings. I was a good walker, I wandered
all over the hills on my own. I knew I could do the
job and a pound a day was a fortune. I'd have loads
to spare, I could buy Mum some Evening in Paris
scent, and humbugs for Grandad.

Better not try the front gate, I thought. It
looked awful posh, so I went round to the back.
It squeaked open and I was smothered in big
black dogs. They were everywhere.

'What d'you want young 'un?' said a gruff old
gardener, straightening himself up from the
cabbages.

'To see Mrs Lawson, mister. About grouse
beating.'

'I'll beat thee if you don't clear off, you little tyke. Anyroads, Lady of the Hall's too busy.'

A large door with big black studs on it opened at the back of the house. A very smart lady appeared, dressed in what looked like her Sunday best, sort of heather-coloured cloth with bits of green and purple. 'What's the young boy want, Harold?' asked the lady.

'Can't make moss 'n sand of him, Ma'am. First he wants to comeon the beating, then he's going on about an evening in Paris.'

'Sounds like humbug,' said the lady.

'Aye,' says Harold, 'well, he'd just got round to mentioning them.'

Harold went off, muttering to the cabbages, and I was beckoned to the house. I approached, stumbling over the black dogs. 'Come inside,' she said, 'let's see if we can sort this out.' She had a friendly voice and made me feel a bit more at ease.

I followed her through the big door with the studs, down a long corridor with a high ceiling and into the biggest room I'd ever seen. A log fire flickered around the walls. Two piercing eyes glared at me from the middle of the floor. It wasn't that Mrs Lawson had suddenly changed from being friendly, just that I'm not used to bumping into tigers. And this one was a fierce-looking one, but thankfully someone had squashed it.

'The Punjab,' muttered Mrs Lawson with a faraway look in her eye. 'It was a long time ago.' I poked it gingerly.

As we got down to business, a young girl brought in a tea tray and a plate of shortcake biscuits. She put them down, nodded her frilly cap and left. I picked up my cup. It rattled on the saucer and kept on rattling. Mrs Lawson was nice. She said she'd been eleven once and seeing as I'd managed to get into the big house maybe I'd be as good at sneaking up on grouse. We got on champion but she told me to let her know if I found all the walking on the moor too much for me. I assured her I wouldn't let her down. I was hired.

Once outside the house Harold made it quite plain that I was a cheeky so-and-so and would never last a day on the moors. 'Anyway,' he said, 'get here half past seven sharp on Wednesday with something to eat and something to sup and wellies or boots. Likely or not it'll be pouring.'

Come Wednesday, Harold was right. It was sheeting down as I peered around the big gate into the courtyard. Everything was chaos. Cars and dogs everywhere, posh blokes in tweeds, ladies in service, guns in leather cases, satchels of cartridges. It was a new world. They might call them gentry but some seemed to swear as much as Grandad.

'What's this?' said a big lad from the group of about thirty beaters, pointing at me.

'It's that little tyke Harold was on about,' said another. 'He'll not last the day. Chuck him into the back of one of the Land Rovers.'

I was jammed into the back of a Land Rover with loads of dogs scrambling all over me, and what were called bird hampers. Seemed to me we were going to feed them rather than shoot them.

Everybody started piling into the posh cars. Mrs Lawson's son, Michael, was in charge, getting everything organised. The gamekeeper was George, a giant of a man. When most of the Lords and Majors were loaded up, I heard Michael telling George, 'Rough Close today if the mist clears.' With that the convoy set off and two of the hampers came crashing down on to me. There were sniggers from the chaps sat in the front.

Between the hampers I could see the track. We trundled away, bouncing around, higher and higher up on to the moors and into the mist. It seemed to take ages. At last we jolted to a stop. 'Right we're here,' gruffed the driver. 'Out you get, tyke.'

Five dogs leaped over me as I fell out of the back. Looking up from the ground all I could see were misty shapes moving about. There was a barn with two doors. They called it The Lodge. It had a posh end for the gentry and an end for us. George was chatting with Michael, then he started dishing out some sticks with white flags on to us beaters.

With a 'Come on, lads' we were off, following George in a line along the edge of the moor. It was a bit of a track and not bad walking. This seemed easy money until we changed direction and went up the moor towards the horizon.

Suddenly I got a nudge in the back. At last someone I knew, it was John who lived near us. 'What happens next, John?' I asked, as I stumbled through deeper heather.

'George will line us up soon, about fifty yards apart, up along the Ghyll. When he gives the signal we'll walk the moor to the line of shooting butts about two miles back, driving up the grouse. Then it's up to them.'

George started dropping folk off, just as John said, and at last it was my turn. 'Right, tyke,' said George, 'stay here, wait for the signal, then move forward. And don't forget – stay in line.'

The rest of them moved off again, lining out higher up the moor until they vanished into the mist. I sat down on a mossy boulder and looked around. I could just make out someone below me and an old man above me lighting his pipe. Waves of mist kept blowing across. It was eerie. Springy heather growing through the spongy, sodden peat gave off a dank smell. All was quiet.

Then, 'C'mon, tyke,' shouts the man with the pipe, waving his flag furiously. 'We're off.'

I started moving. The heather was thick but it was awfully boggy in parts. I tripped again, which made three times already and something went in my wellies. Then there were some grouse. I could just make them out, crouching ever so still, just by that ... 'Back, tyke, down, down,' screamed the old man as a covey of grouse lifted and veered over me – in the wrong direction.

The beat carried on. My enthusiasm was tempered by the fifty birds they blamed me for losing. Then I heard shots in the distance. Sort of putt-putt noises. Something was happening. I tripped again, smashed my stick and both wellies came off. We were close to the butts, though, because I could see the shooters as I looked up from the heather.

Grouse were skimming the moor, hugging the ground, fast and wheeling. Wonderful things. Then a flurry of down as one fell from the sky like an exploding feather pillow. There were sharp

whistles as we neared the shooters. Dogs were running out to collect the dead birds. 'Blanche, away, away. Good dog.' There was lots of noise.

'What a blinking mess,' said the old man, eyeing me up and down, 'but at least you kept up, so we'll say nothing of them birds you sent to Arncliffe.'

There were two more beats that morning and I seemed to do a little better. By dinnertime the bag was down and so were faces. They'd only shot twenty pairs of birds. They called them braces – like I had for my trousers.

I stayed outside The Lodge on my own, eating my butties, knowing this would be my first and last day. I wandered around, giving myself something to remember. There were the grouse laid out in twos. George was checking which were old and which were young birds. He could tell by their flight feathers or their beak.

The gentry were tucking into a real feast. I'd never seen anything like it – hams and meats and bottles of drinks all laid out on linen tablecloths. And also carefully laid out were the guns. Two especially caught my eye. I daren't touch but they seemed exactly the same, even the silver engraving. Everything about them was beautifully made.

There was a tap on my shoulder. It was George. 'Them, my lad, are a matching pair of Purdeys. You'll see guns like that perhaps once in a lifetime, and if you don't fare a bit better this afternoon, that's not going to be right long is it?'

I dreaded the afternoon coming. Best I could hope for was to get shot. But not too shot, just enough so they'd still need to pay me.

We lined up again, fifty yards apart, and I was right on the top of a steep ridge. The rest of the line was beneath me and George was still dropping others off along the ridge top. It would take another fifteen or twenty minutes before we'd be ready. The mist was down again but as I sat down preparing myself for the wait, it cleared, just enough for me to see John sitting fifty yards below me.

I gave him a quick wave and a smile. The message was relayed like through a line of dominoes and thirty beaters beneath me moved forward. God, I wished I'd got a gun and I wouldn't have needed two barrels. My half of the beaters were advancing at a rapid rate through the moor, before an astonished George's half had even set off.

Covey after covey of grouse stirred up by my lot went wheeling up the ridge. There were hundreds of birds, like flocks of starlings. Then the pincer movement we created had a dramatic effect (or perhaps George's face was enough) and the birds all veered back down, straight into the line of guns.

When at last I got to the butts, it was like a battlefield. Everyone had armfuls of grouse and scores of spent cartridge cases. Come home time we got an extra ten bob apiece. 'See you same time on Friday, tyke,' said George, 'and there's just room for you in this Merc.'

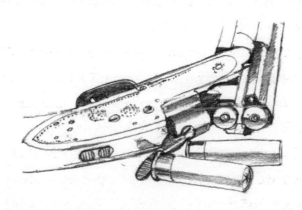

Soul for all Seasons

꩜

Women in pinnies and headscarves, and tin baths hanging outside ready for Friday nights. These unchanging signs said that things were well down our back street. So with mucky fingers stained with kali, us kids got on with our games. The fells provided the biggest backyard in the world. It was a child's paradise. We never stopped till tiredness took us home. Only the seasons ruled us.

Spring meant longer days; catkins coming out, the first bunch of primroses and cowslips collected from the railway banking and armfuls of bluebells. The fields were covered with carpets of bloodied daisies – till they unfurled their starry white petals. Blackthorn and hawthorn

gave way to sticky buds as the chestnut candles opened up, and Satan's bread provided the ammunition for our peashooters. We drank endless bottles of Spanish water, painted Easter eggs and built dens. A prized cob of lime, dropped from the quarry wagon, marked out the hopscotch. If you'd drawn it, it was yours, but everything else was shared.

Waterhens, a flash of a kingfisher, ducks with families, dippers and yellowhammers bobbed up and down by the river where we went to catch minnow and bullheads. We saw trout and grayling and hatches of mayfly, gobbled up by the ripples. Chasing through the buttercups in our mothballed cossies, we were ready to explore a new season.

We learned to swim in Devil's Pool. We believed that the Devil lived under the ledge at the deep end. We laid on it and peered under; it was frightening. Above Devil's Pool was the weir. Monkey flowers grew on its mossy sides. Some days the water came over the weir, smooth as glass. We'd stand behind it and hunt for crayfish. Above the weir, where the big boys swam, it was deep. We called it the six-foot end; that was as deep as we could imagine. They had a raft up there made from an old door and four Castrol oil drums. Sometimes we'd get a ride on it.

Summer drifted into early autumn. We didn't need a calendar to tell us when the first mushrooms were ready. We sold them in paper bags at the roadside. Grandma didn't like me charging for them but, as I told her, I was doing folk a service because they'd never find any for themselves.

The conkers ripened and split open as they hit the ground. We'd get our sticks stuck up the tree trying to knock them down and then have to search for another one suitable for the task.

When at last the nights drew in, the back street reigned supreme. It had lights and lampposts – somewhere to gather and swing. Holes in the road served well for games with blood alleys and marbles. And round the lamppost we made our plans for Bonfire Night.

We always seemed to be at school when the first white flakes came down. Everybody would be looking towards the windows, hoping it wouldn't stop before playtime. After school we rushed home to get our sledges, old wooden things with rusty runners. Then we were down the field tops, sledging till it was dark. My fingers tingled painfully when I got back into the warm. When at last in bed, it was an uneasy sleep with the excitement of Christmas so close.

Lumpy Custard

෴

It was summertime, and the peonies were out. The postman came up the path of our front garden. For the last few days, I'd been peering round the curtain every morning about ten past eight watching for him. He always whistles; I thought, that's why they call him Ronnie Merry.

I knew the letter would look official when it finally came, probably in a long white envelope. Mum heard the letterbox slam as it fell to the floor. She opened it, pondered a while and looked over at me. The bacon sizzled in the pan. 'Terry,' she said, her face expressionless, 'you're on probation.'

I'd heard that word before, seen it in the local paper. It meant something to do with the police.

But I hadn't done anything wrong! I'd tried my best, my very best. And it hadn't been easy.

'What's it mean, Mum?' I asked, cautiously.

'It means you'll have to try hard because if they find you're not good enough you'll leave the school. Then you'd have to go to the Secondary and the best you could hope for would be the paper mill or quarry when you left.'

Where I lived you had the chance of sitting the entrance exam for the local public school at Giggleswick. It was around the same time as the Eleven Plus exam. Most of the lads who went there were boarders because they came from away. A local old gentleman had left money so that us village lads could also be given the chance if we were clever enough to pass the entrance exam.

I remembered the day of that test. There were eight of us. We walked over to the school together. We had to be there by ten o'clock. A lady came to the door of the Headmaster's house, next to the school, and showed us into a long room with desks and chairs. We were asked to sit down. She gave us all a piece of paper with sums on and told us to get as far as we could with them. She said that while we were getting on with that, she'd take each of us in turn into another room to meet Mr Ainsworth. He would tell us to read something from a book and ask a few questions. She left, taking one of the boys with her.

I looked around the room. It was threatening and cold with stern, gnarled oak beams, a heavy smell of Mansion furniture polish and heartless lino.

Why arithmetic? Why couldn't they ask me about things that I knew? More important things like where to find slipper orchids on the moors, how to make a Greenwell's Glory for fly-fishing. I looked back to the question on the paper. I stared and stared and thought and thought. I had to pass. It was important.

Uncle John lived next door to us. He was bedfast now but he'd been a day boy at the school. Very clever was Uncle John, and he knew where the orchids were as well. I couldn't see the questions so well. They were going all blurred. Everybody at home was crossing their fingers for me and here I was messing it up.

'Terry Wilson,' said the lady, 'your turn to see the Headmaster now.' She led me into a room she called the study. It was huge with a big desk, chairs and a sofa, and a gigantic cheese plant straining for light. 'Sit over here please, Terry,' said a deep voice.

The Headmaster stood up. He had a black coat on and he was enormous. He handed me a book. It was *Moby Dick*. I was told to read the passage that he'd marked. I started okay but the further I got, the shakier my voice became. 'What's wrong?' asked the Headmaster in a friendly way. It all came out and I told him everything.

'And that's not all, I want to win the Rigg Race.' That was the annual cross-country race for the older boys at the school. It was famous. 'I run everywhere I go,' I said. 'I like running but I can't do fractions. I need lots of apples and a penknife to see how big the bits add up. And if the numbers are big I run out of apples.' My voice broke again.

Mr Ainsworth sat back and roared. He started asking me about things I like to do. He seemed to understand. Eventually he said, 'Well you can go back now, Terry. Don't let those questions upset you. You can only try your best. Remember, that's all you can ever do.' That phrase was to live with me all my days at the school.

So there it was. Mr Ainsworth had sent the long white envelope saying he'd put me on probation for a year. Now he was somebody else I hadn't got to let down!

It was a new world for me as I pedalled off that first morning to start at prep school. I looked down at my new bike and saddlebag which all the parents bought their sons if they managed to get to that school. I'd also noticed that Grandad had stopped smoking.

I felt uneasy but I waved back as a proud family watched me turn the corner. Grandma wiped a tear. 'Not the gasworks for him,' Grandad muttered. Mum now had something special to talk about at the paper mill that morning.

I'd often seen the lads in blue jackets and red caps. Now I was one. As I went over the river bridge I thought I'll be doing this for two years till I go to the big school. But I'd lots of things to learn first.

It was a mile and a half to the school. I started to meet other boys on bikes with the same jacket and caps. Some were older, some new like me and some I'd known from my old school. There were occasional friendly faces.

It was a few hundred yards up the posh drive to the school. It had a stream and a waterfall. I noticed a trout dart back under a ledge as we passed and that made me feel better. There was an easy banter between the older boys. We new ones said little as we walked into the unknown.

As we grappled with life for the first few weeks so much was new. The day boys, there on scholarships, were called day dogs by the boarders. Because their parents had paid for them, boarders had common rooms to go to when there were no lessons, where they would make model aeroplanes and things. We had to make do with empty classrooms, pushing desks together to make table tennis tables, playing shove ha'penny and things like that. Every day after lunch we had a quiet hour. Everyone had to go to the common room or get a book from the library and read. I didn't like that. I'd only liked *William* books. I had lots of those at home but they didn't have any at school. But another book I'd read at home was *King Solomon's Mines*. I liked that so I put it in the library and got it out every time.

The boarders also had a matron with a white pinny. She looked after them when they had problems. That seemed fair as their families were a long way away. They also had tuck boxes and big trunks with metal hoops round them, somewhere to keep their private things.

The school had its own vicar. His name was Mr Clegg but he was called Padre. The day boys liked him as he bought us table tennis bats and balls and Monopoly sets out of his own money. But he still shouted at us in lessons if we didn't try. I had a lot of respect for him.

The whole day revolved around bells. You had to learn the system or you were never where you should be. Then you'd be in trouble. It was all too easy to get lost in those corridors, struggling with armfuls of heavy books.

The best bell was meal times. Again, there was a difference. Boarders had two dining rooms while we had 'the hut'. A master sat at the top of the table and the red-cheeked Padre was the head of ours. One of us would fetch the tray of food from the hatch or a maid would bring it and Mr Clegg divided it up. We passed the plates down the long table but we couldn't start till he'd said the Grace in Latin.

The wooden table was all greasy. It had seen a lot of gravy and spuds over the years. They scrubbed it now and again but the food won. Macaroni cheese, shepherd's pie and haslet were most common. Anything simple that went a long way. I wondered what the boarders thought to the food. I bet they had chicken at home. The puddings, which I loved, were usually tubes of sponge with lashings of lumpy custard. Stodge, as we called the pudding, came in different varieties – whitish, brown, brown with currants and chocolate. Mr Clegg cut the tubes into slices and passed it down. There was always a good chance for seconds of stodge and back went my plate whenever seconds were called.

At morning break it was milk and stidgers. Stidgers were an institution, a simple dough bun like a roll, made for more years than anyone could remember by Mr Rushton in the village baker's shop. Long wooden trays of steaming-hot stidgers came every morning on the dot at break-time. We'd line up and get one apiece, a valuable commodity as you could barter with stidgers. A boy called Holden seemed lonely. He was a boarders' outcast perhaps because he had flaky skin, but I found him interesting to talk to, and what's more, he didn't like stidgers! I saved my second stidger for later in the day.

Games were played most afternoons. Cricket in summer, football in autumn and rambles in the countryside in winter. Wooden boards with pegs hung in the main corridor and were called sets. Our names were glued on to a peg in one of the sets. That became your set, your team and your position. Boys in the first set were best, those in the eighth worst. I quickly made the eighth set in every sport.

Cricket balls hurt when you're watching swallows swooping. Wet footballs are heavy. But winter rambles I excelled in. I showed the others the secret dew ponds on the limestone scars. They took their model racing cars and ran them around the dried-up pond. I'd show them sights they'd never seen. They mellowed and I held my position, even though it wasn't reflected by my sets.

The highlight of the year was Bonfire Night. It was wonderful. The boarders competed to bring the best fireworks and we held it in the Ghyll Field which had been an old musket range hundreds of years ago. We often dug old musket balls out of the banking. When we were digging we'd also find pig nuts which we scoffed. As our fireworks lit the sky and masters rushed about lighting them, we ate parkin. My friends from home sat on the Ghyll Field wall watching our bonfire. I had my red cap on and gumboots but they still wore wellies and had holes in their pullies.

As I rode home on my bike at night, it sometimes felt strange. Our worlds were very different and I was afraid we'd lose touch.

PART TWO

Uncle John

〜

After I'd finished my supper I'd go and sit next door with Uncle John. He'd be laid in his bed in the front room and I'd sit in the chair by the window. Now and again a moonbeam lit up part of his face. I often wondered how it had come to this. It seemed such a waste.

We talked for hours, Uncle John and I. He was a simple man. He was bedfast, muscles wasting with muscular dystrophy, but it didn't affect his mind. I'd seen faded brown photos of when he was young. He and Grandma, who was his sister, came from a large, poor family, brought up in the railway cottages at Alton. I knew of his candlelit struggles to get to Cambridge University, of his extraordinary success as history master at a Sheffield Grammar School and of the ill-health which brought early retirement.

We'd looked after him for years and Grandma did most of it. A door was made between our two cottages. Every morning things were taken in for his morning shave, together with a white pint pot of tea and a slice of toast. The time had to be eight o'clock, not earlier, not later. If he didn't say anything we knew it wasn't eight o'clock.

As Uncle John stropped his cut-throat razor, Grandma emptied the ashes from the fire. It was closed in with perspex to make it safe and had two little doors that opened. He always made the same comment. 'Don't put the poker through the windows. It needs a quarter-inch draught and give it a good scuffle.' He was totally predictable. No reply was necessary, it simply signified that the day had begun. 'Clock needs winding,' he'd say then. 'Not too much, don't over-wind it.' Usually Grandma put the key in and gave it a few turns. Every turn creaked. I shivered when I did it.

Uncle John would finish with the shaving water and sit on the edge of the bed partly dressed in his waistcoat and jacket. Last of all he put on his flat cap, just in case Jesus made him right again, he said. Then he'd straighten the pompoms that hung from his lapel. I'd made them from milkbottle tops and wool at a time when I'd been knee high and fascinated by his stories about Brer Fox and Brer Rabbit.

Then he sat at his little table. It was very small but he could write on it. All his possessions were to hand, including the yellow *Wisden's Cricket Almanacs*. He could tell you who'd hit what in every over in every test mach for years. I thought they were good books as they were thick and stopped everything else falling off the table.

More importantly, my matchbox appeared beside the Almanacs on Fridays. Fridays were specially good days to wind his clock up. By the side of Captain Webb on the matchbox were the pencilled initials T.W. I'd be given the box and inside would be a little parcel wrapped up in the silver paper from his Digger Flake tobacco. It was my pocket money.

He used to get a lot of letters from people but rarely saw anyone. He liked it when Jed Proctor, the local gamekeeper, came visiting because they would talk for hours about the old times and the moors.

Sometimes one of his old boys knocked on our back door and asked to see Uncle John. They had a lot of respect for him, they said that everyone had mattered to him, that he'd been an inspired master and a friend. He never compromised his simple background. In winter he'd worn a shawl as well as his flat cap. He was their original Mr Chips.

One man told me he was the British Commissioner in Kuala Lumpur. I nearly dropped. As we entered Uncle John said, 'Sit down, Smith Minor.' I crawled out. He didn't like them bringing presents, he said it wasn't necessary, but he would accept a Dutch cheese or a bottle of Cherry Heering at Christmas. He liked a bit of cheese at night and the drink warmed him up.

You'd have thought with Uncle John's history background I'd have passed history at GCE but

I didn't and it was his fault. I never knew enough dates of things. He said dates stopped people learning about history and didn't really matter. It was how people lived and what they felt that was important. He told me a lot about the Romans and Greeks and brought it all to life.

Suddenly, at seventy years of age, he got interested in science. He'd never done any before. One night he asked, 'What do you know about laser beams?' I sat bolt upright. 'Not done them yet,' I said. He went quiet.

That was the start of the science books arriving and each night he soaked up every bit of science I knew. The teacher/pupil roles were reversed.

He had a distinct advantage on me as he was studying eight hours a day and I only had chemistry and physics twice a week. When I couldn't answer a question he asked me to mention it to the science master at class. Trouble was it was always more advanced stuff than what we were doing. Eventually I had to come clean and explain to the master about Uncle John. Then everyone gained.

Whenever Uncle John had a question I brought it to the science master and it became the homework for that night. Everyone liked the change and it made people think. Bedfast and seventy, he still influenced the way things were taught.

One day he told me to listen very carefully. He explained the arrangements to follow his death. The list was comprehensive, the instructions simple and plain; the people to write to, even the card we were to send out and the notice for Lambert's paper shop window. Everything was put into a small leather writing case and when the day came that I had to open it, I found he'd also written his own epitaph.

I put a simple headstone on Uncle John's grave with a message that I thought best summed him up. It was in Latin, the language we had shared so often. His old friend Mr Frankland and the vicar nodded approvingly, they knew what it meant. *Res Amantiquae Amavit* – a lover of the old way of life.

Encyclopaedia Britannica

༄

Now we'd see how good these books were. This would be their first real test. Grandma had fallen into the trap of a door-to-door salesman. Twenty-four volumes of *Encyclopaedia Britannica* stood in our kitchen, just delivered, with a smell of new leather and a bill to pay over the centuries.

In the country you make your own amusements. I picked out the one that said GUNN to HYDROX and scampered off upstairs. Grandma smiled at my keenness to learn.

There were pages and pages about gunpowder, and best of all the formula. This had endless possibilities. I studied the list of ingredients but where was I going to get that lot from? Then came a brainwave. I knew where I could get the first from but I'd have to be up in the morning before Grandad. I closed the book and went downstairs.

'I'm going fishing early in the morning,' I announced, 'so I'll light the fire for you, Grandad, before I go.'

'Tha's a good lad,' said Grandad, concentrating on his Littlewood's football coupon and his vision of owning an ice-cream shop. He always said we'd be partners if it ever happened.

Morning came. I was into my trousers and jumper and downstairs as quick as I could. Now for the fireplace, nice and cold, with a whole chimney full of ingredient number one – soot.

A paper bag from the pantry and the hearth brush and I was away, reaching up as far as I could. But I didn't get much. That was Grandad's fault. He always cleaned off what he could before he lit the fire. I needed something longer. The yard brush! It wasn't easy getting it past the bend but it went up. Well, it did till it stuck. I was pulling and tugging, rattling about, and all of a sudden the light went out – caused by a whole year's supply of ingredient one!

With Bobby the budgie choking to death and inches of soot everywhere, a fast excuse was needed. I was out of the back door and over the wall. Two gardens down I yanked an old crow off the pea sticks, rushed back to the house and hurled it into the hearth.

'What's going on?' came from the top of the stairs.

'It's a crow, Grandad. Stuck up the chimney. It's brought all the soot down.' Phew. It said in the book that making gunpowder is tricky and they were right.

I'd seen the next two ingredients somewhere, I couldn't think where, but I knew they were together on a shelf. Then I remembered. My friend Johnnie's dad had them in his greenhouse. Flowers of sulphur and saltpetre. He used them for his prize chrysanths and dahlias.

Johnnie became a willing partner. What's more, his dad had a shed adjoining their greenhouse which provided somewhere to experiment. He offered the opinion that the *Encyclopaedia Britannica* had got it wrong, suggesting that some sugar and weedkiller might help. So we gave it a go. At last we were ready to mix according to the book plus the extras. One dollop of sugar and two dollops of weedkiller were inspired guessworks so we placed a small pile on the bench to test it. I offered Johnnie a match seeing as it was his shed. He declined the offer as it was my idea. In true Western style I trickled a thin line of powder along the bench, smiled confidently at Johnnie and put the match to it. It fizzed along, then there was a big poof, a flash of lightning and smoke everywhere. We did a quick jig. Good stuff, this education. Now, what next?

We looked around the shed. An old bike pump would do. With the inside taken out we had a perfect cannon. We half filled it with powder, then twenty bicycle ball bearings, a wad of newspaper and we were ready. Johnnie put it into the vice and aimed it at an old wooden box on the end of the bench.

This time it was Johnnie's turn. I peered around the doorway as he lit the touch-paper. It fired instantly. Johnnie flew back without moving his legs. I could hear bells and it wasn't Sunday. The splintering of wood seemed a sure sign of success.

I dragged the dazed Johnnie back into the fog. He didn't look happy with our success. But there was a box in smithereens. A direct hit. Unfortunately, three yards further on was the wooden greenhouse door, neatly peppered with ball bearings.

'Wood filler and paint,' I said, 'your dad won't even know.'

'Okay,' said Johnnie, 'but how are we going to get the heads back on thirty-odd chrysanths?'

I suppose banning us from the shed didn't seem unduly harsh under the circumstances. So we decided to go underground – in more senses than one. It took a long time to get the crowbar four feet down at the bottom end of the lawn. It was my turn to light this one so I'd prepared a piece of rope soaked in paraffin. It seemed like a clever idea.

There was a heavy thud as the powder went up. We were left with a dome-shaped lawn, three feet higher in the middle than the sides. We stood and stared. Then it got worse as the turf slowly sank back and went corrugated.

෧

No longer welcome on this earth, there was only one thing left for us to try – space. The fells above the quarry, a good mile away from the village, would provide an ideal launch site. Learning from past experience we slowed the mixture down and at last she was ready. Our rocket. Her name took some choosing but we settled for MIRACLE painted along the sides in red. It was a proud moment when I took our three-foot-long beauty out of an old golf bag and positioned her on a flat lump of limestone. She gleamed in the sunlight.

It was a responsible launch. I looked down on the valley below me, then checked for a gap between overhead planes at thirty thousand feet. She lifted beautifully, orange smoke pouring from behind. Then for some reason she levelled out at about five hundred feet and headed like a racing pigeon for home; across the quarry, over the road, down the golf course and straight for the village. Through my binoculars, I could see Johnnie leaping about in his garden.

The explosion happened somewhere between the church and the vicarage. Estimated height –

one hundred feet. The only bit they found caused quite a stir. It said IRA. It was time to stop our experiments.

The Old Tramp

~

You don't see tramps today, not the real ones. Wasters or scroungers they'd be called now but it wasn't always like that. The first time I used the word 'tramp', Grandma nearly knocked me into next week. 'Gentlemen of the Road, they are, Terry, remember that. It's only their way. They can't settle.'

There seemed to be a place for Gentlemen of the Road in those days and they had a respect in society. They did odd jobs for a mug of tea or a bite to eat or maybe a bob for a pint. And often they'd ask for a bowl of hot water for a wash. The few belongings they had were in an old bag but all carefully wrapped in brown paper. They were very private people but they remembered a kindness.

They didn't scrounge and they gave back all they could; a bag of mushrooms left at the back door or some herbs 'for the missus's chest'.

We recognised old faces when they arrived in the village for a day or two. They'd visit, do the odd job, exchange a few words, not many, and off again until next year. We saw nature take its toll in their faces as years rolled on; the bad chest developing, the arthritis setting in. Inevitably a year would go by and one of them hadn't been around.

Jim was like that. It was always June and it was like an old friend coming home. It was nice to see him come down the back street in the old brown trilby he wore even when asleep. 'Jim's back, Grandma,' I'd tell her.

He used the old hut at the back of our house. To have a roof over his head was a rare, uneasy treat for him. He loved Grandma's jam pasty and rock buns but he always carried his own pint pot for a brew. It was near black on the inside from use over the years. 'Seasoned,' said Jim. He wouldn't let us clean it. 'Just rinse it,' he said, 'it tastes better.'

He was best at chopping firewood and he also sharpened knives on his stone. I'd sit and watch him. It was a grand sight on a summer's day. The lads on the back street would peer around the corner at Jim, then scamper off before Old Nick caught them. He didn't frighten me, though, and now and again he'd say a bit of something or give an infrequent smile.

We had an old chair in the hut. He sat there in the doorway when he'd done his work, near motionless, like the tattooed man in *Moby Dick* – waiting to die. I'd watch him, peering to see if his chest was still moving. Then a bit of smoke would wisp from his lips, drawn from his old clay pipe. I liked Jim.

Uncle John always looked forward to June; it was always special when Jim came. Before he got bedfast he'd sit with Jim in the doorway and Jim would tell him of his year in the countryside, where he'd been and anything that had happened. I had to run up to Lizzie Cox's shop for an ounce of black twist. He always shared it with Jim.

The year Uncle John died Jim came around as usual. He didn't know about Uncle John or that the cottage had been left to me. I was only a lad and we hadn't the heart at the time to do anything with it so we'd just left his cottage as it was. Grandma smiled and nodded when I asked if Jim could stay at Uncle John's for a couple of days.

I never went inside Uncle John's while Jim was there. You trust folk or you don't. I went in after he'd left and next to an old photo of Uncle John was a jar of fresh wild flowers, half an ounce of black twist and the old penknife they'd shared.

Haytiming

❧

As a young lad I learned the three things you need to know about farmers. They work hard, they eat like kings and they won't part with their brass. They have a simple philosophy. When they're selling anything it's scarce, best quality or fetching top money. When they're buying it's always too dear.

Now there was one thing I had that they needed, at least every haytiming. My two strong arms. The first year I did it was an economic disaster. Full of zip I'd been, but what did I get out of it? A full stomach, loads of brews and the odd bottle of beer. Reflecting on it, I hadn't gained much.

As I opened the gate to Lingwood House Farm I wondered what old farmer Lister would think to my idea for this year's haytiming. It had the hall-mark of genius. I'd work harder than anybody, I'd get something money couldn't buy, I'd be a land-owner of sorts – and it'd cost him nothing. He'd like that.

'Price of land's dear, Mr Lister,' I said, as he straightened his cowclapped gaiters in the yard.

'Aye, lad,' he said reflecting, 'they've stopped making it!'

I tightened up my act. Farmers can be unbelievably disarming. 'I'd like some land, Mr Lister,' I said. At that he went stone deaf. 'Rabbits,' I persisted, 'somewhere to shoot rabbits. Bet they eat lots of your grass?'

I came at him from two sides. It'd cost him nowt and I'd help get his hay in – and, what's more, there'd be more of it with less rabbits. His eyes twitched. He looked up from his gaiters. 'Stick thee hand out,' he chortled, 'it's a deal. Thar can shoot Lingwood for a year.' He cracked my hand like at auction. I'd got my first forty acres!

The formula worked well. Within two years I had one thousand eight hundred and six acres on farms all over the place. But of all those places, Lingwood House, where it had all started, was my favourite.

Haytiming at Lingwood had stopped halfway through the industrial revolution. This meant that once a machine had stopped a few times and no one could fix it, then it went into the little field by the house. The pile of rusting, rotting machinery grew every year, and when the field was full they knocked down a wall to expand!

It was a house full of characters. Mrs Lister was everyone's grandma. Every delight imaginable appeared on the long farmhouse table after our day's work. The hired hands sat along the benches, tucking into her beef and pickles, home-cured hams, with mugs of tea and a drop of ale to wash it all down.

Evenings were times for reflection and planning but there was a lot of looking back and not so much looking forward. Like, how come when we'd got to Mearbank Meadow the first day, the baler twine in the machine was still there from last year and had gone rotten? Why did Dick make bales so tight and heavy, it took two of us to lift one? There'd been a near revolution from the men as Dick, oblivious to the world, belted around the meadow on his tractor leaving immovable bales in his wake. How come Dick's corduroy trousers were glued to the tractor seat except for meal times? And why had he decided to bale a field a few miles away while ten men and two empty trailers waited patiently in a different field, with Mr Lister jumping up and down scanning the horizon?

Mr Lister had two tractors and it was not unusual for us to be on the way to pick up bales in one tractor, on a single-track lane, and meet Dick returning in the other one. It was like a two-tractor Mexican showdown. You could hear the argument all round the valley. 'Lingwood's started haytiming again!' someone in the village would astutely observe.

The Foss

❦

I rarely go there now. Just sometimes in a hard winter to see the frozen waterfall or in the autumn to watch the golden leaves drift down on to the water. Those are the best times when no one else is about. It brings back memories and above all respect. It's the perfect picture postcard. The river flows under the old horse bridge at Stainforth and down three waterfalls. The bottom one is the Foss. If you look on a map it's called Stainforth Force but you aren't going to convince locals of that.

It's deep, black and bottomless; a hole with sheer cliffs on two sides and trees going up through the sky. The sun never warms it, not even in summer. It's a siren, it lures people and that's always been the problem. If you were in trouble, as men have been over the years, that's where you'd go on a cold January night and we'd never see you again. After a few days they'd drag the Foss. It happened so many times.

Ducky Wildman's dad used to ride an old bike out of the wood, just managing to get off before it hit the water. He was the attraction all that summer. So was the rope dangling temptingly from the tree over the Foss. Many's the Tarzan who tangled his toes. Their yells echoed around the walls.

A summer sun would see a young man fluttering, to his new love on the banks of the Foss in his first posh cossie, the first sprouts of hair on his chest. He'd jump from the wood down into the Foss, bubbles and bubbles came up, then at last he'd surface – a warrior. The girl would turn away, chatter to other girls, pretend not to notice. But you knew they'd be going together now.

It didn't always happen just like that. Sometimes blood came up from a belly ripped open on the Foss's hidden teeth.

Nowadays, some of the tourists take an hour to put on their black rubber suits, sloshed in talc and watched by the crowd. They haven't all returned. Anyway none of them are as good as Ducky's dad.

The Cauli

⨑

Edna was a pensioner who lived a few doors down from us. Grandad always grew veg in her garden and we shared the produce with her. But now Grandad reckoned he was too old for gardening so it was time for me to take over.

'I won't interfere,' said Grandad, 'but you're setting those caulis too far apart.' I looked up from the soil and thought of the time he'd grown a two-pound King Edward potato. It had won the local show and he'd told that story for years to anyone who'd listen. 'They'll need room,' I said. 'I want to grow some big ones. There's a barrow-load of muck under each stick and that's where the cauli plants are going.'

'Waste of good muck,' said Grandad, 'you don't grow good caulis round here.' He wandered off, muttering.

Well, that did it. His Irish background was showing through again and my Northern grit wasn't about to be trod on. Trouble was, all I knew then was that the shoot goes to the top, the roots to the bottom, and I'd overheard someone saying caulis loved muck.

The next few weeks I asked about, read about, talked about and thought about nothing but caulis. I'd see Grandad at meal times but he never came round to Edna's. I did like it said in an old gardening book – 'Turn the leaves over the middle to protect the curd and loosely tie them up.' Then the hot dry spell came and it was two gallons of water for each cauli each day. The drought lasted a fortnight, right up to the day before the show.

Friday night, with the show the following day, was the time of truth. I turned round Edna's path to the back garden, wishing I'd been to church on Sunday, took my penknife out and cut the string holding in the first cauli. It unfurled. Grandad's stick came tapping around the corner. My eyes lifted up, went steely, then looked back down to a cauli the size of a saucer. Hopefully expressionless, I moved to the second of the six. Same again, maybe a little bigger. The third and the fourth were the same. As I cut the fifth Grandad picked up his stick which rested against the wall, muttered, 'Told you so' and disappeared.

With a vicious swipe I cut the string on the fifth – and blimey, it was as big as you get on the market. It must have a chance. Nearly as an afterthought I leaned over and cut the string of the last one. I stared and stared at it. Nearly eighteen inches across and pure white. I gave a quick wink to heaven, tied the leaves back over and whistling 'All Things Bright and Beautiful' scampered home for tea.

The morning of the show was quite exciting. A bit daunting too. A lot of old-timers there knew me but they didn't connect me with gardening, not a kid. They were all busy rushing around laying out their veg on the tables and probably thought I was helping with the chairs.

To keep it white, my cauli was wrapped up in last week's *Weekly Herald*, inside a cardboard box. I clutched it tighter, walked past the peas, onions and beans and stopped at the cauli section. I scanned the entries with a jumping heart and a slight smile. There were none as big as mine and none as white as mine. There was just one problem: they'd have to push theirs up

THIRD PRIZE

Terry Wilson

a bit if I was to get mine on the table. The trouble was, I daren't ask anybody or they'd think I was being cheeky.

'Five minutes to go,' shouted somebody with a badge that said STEWARD, 'then all out ready for judging.'

That'll do, I thought, if I wait till they've all gone I can shove 'em up a bit and get mine on. So that's what I did, though it meant cutting all the leaves off to fit it in. But it looked magnificent.

The river sparkled beautifully as I skipped back home over the bridge. They'd be judging it right now. The show opened again in two hours and then I'd know.

Grandma's tatie hash was bubbling on the stove as I came through the back door and we all sat down to eat. 'I think it's the show today,' said Grandad, gumming a piece of meat to death. 'You want to come this year, lad, and maybe you'll learn a bit?' There was a slight Irish snigger in his voice.

'Aye, maybe I'd better,' said I.

It was a grand feeling as we both set off over the river bridge. Grandad was treated with a bit of reverence when we got to the show. They hadn't forgotten his two-pound King Edward.

'Chip off the old block, Jakie. See you learned him a bit,' said an old chap puffing away on his twist. Grandad looked puzzled.

'Never seen a cauli like it,' said another fellow as we passed down the line.

'It should have got first prize,' said another old salt.

Now that last remark wasn't funny. There were too many people in front of the caulis to see what was happening. We squeezed through.

'Damn shame,' muttered someone, shaking his head and poking my cauli. It said third prize.

Grandad scanned them. 'Now that, my lad, is a cauli,' he said, pointing to mine. 'Criminal, cutting t'leaves off, though. That's why they've dropped it to third. It could have been best exhibit in the show.'

'It would have been,' said a man leaning over with a badge on saying JUDGE.

'Pass us t'third prize ticket,' said Grandad, 'it'll have his name on. He's a fair grower whoever he is.'

Monster of the Deeps

~

Within two yeas of joining the fishing club I won the president's annual prize for best brown trout. My prize was a Hardy's fly rod, the finest money could buy.

Other parts of the river miles downstream now beckoned to me; Moley's Hole, Rathmell Bottoms, The Deeps. The mysterious names conjured up monsters. Few people went there but I'd heard stories.

It was a long walk. The low lingering mist clung to the river as I made my way along. Eventually the gurgling currents gave way to stillness as if the river had come to an end. Dewy cobwebs hung from reeds. A wild mink sat devouring its catch, glaring at the intrusion. And the rising sun dazzled back from the water and hid the secrets of The Deeps.

The river bank was higher here, potted with the holes of sand martins. A lone figured crouched, peering over the top, and beckoned me to come along the field side of the banking. He was stocky, older than me and wore dark glasses.

He took them off and motioned for me to put them on and the glare of the sunlit surface instantly disappeared. There she lay in eight feet of water, motionless by the swaying reed bed, camouflaged to perfection.

There was a thumping in the ground. A bunch of frisky bullocks clattered down to the water's edge. The monster slipped into the deep blackness and was gone.

He never did catch that pike, nor did I. Yet we saw her one last time. She'd been cast aside on the banking by a salmon fisherman. We slipped her body back into the pool.

Driving Lessons

ᔥ

A woman of vision was Grandma. 'I've had a word with Mr Bradley,' she said. 'He'll show you how to do it but he says you can't start until your birthday in January.' There didn't seem much point to me. We weren't rich enough to own a car, in fact there was only one down our street.

'Mr Bradley's a policeman, Grandma,' I said. 'He's always shouting at us young 'uns – scares the pants off us.' Grandma wouldn't argue. She just said if I was going to learn, I'd learn properly.

My birthday arrived and I sat on the sofa in clean shirt, tie and brushed shoes, wondering why shoe polish always seemed to spray on to your cuffs. This whole business didn't seem a good idea, especially as Flash Gordon was on television on Saturday nights and we'd only had our telly since the previous summer. We'd got it for the Coronation because Grandma was big into royalty. She never missed the opportunity for a good National Anthem. That's why she stayed up till the programmes finished at night and went to the picture house every Saturday – just for the National Anthem.

There was a knock on the back door. It was Mr Bradley. Grandma sat him down on the sofa and I moved to a chair near the television. Grandma opened her brown purse and gave him some money. I couldn't hear all their conversation but Saturday nights for a few weeks was mentioned. My heart sank and my left hand stroked the television as Flash Gordon came on.

'Come on then, Terry,' said Mr Bradley, 'let's make a start.' Grandma saw us off with one of her little waves.

It was raining as we left and I hoped it might put Mr Bradley off, what with the road conditions and the pitch black, but he strode on to the end of the street where his car was parked. There were two cheeky young monkeys hanging around it but his booming voice sent them flying around the Co-op corner. He unlocked the car and I was just about to jump in when he said, 'Wrong seat. It's you that's driving.'

He put on the inside light, pointed out the pedals, told me things to do, then put the lights out. It didn't make much sense but one way or another we set off forward, bouncing round the Co-op corner. I clutched the wheel tighter as we swung on to the main road. Things were getting awfully complicated and Mr Bradley was dragging faster on his Woodbine.

There seemed to be something wrong with the car. It made a heck of a noise when I tried to change the gear for the hilly bits. As the headlights

picked up Buckhaw Brow I couldn't see me and Mr Bradley standing much chance with it. We hadn't got up that hill on the Shed Mill bus outing to Morecambe last year.

Glaring at Buckhaw Brow like it was Everest, determined we'd not be beaten, he lit another Woodbine. The fog in the car was building up rapidly. He started telling me he was leaving the police force because of his nerves and was he doing the right thing? 'Second, second,' he screamed. Then went back to his personal problems.

Eight weekends later I had learned a lot about Mr Bradley and not too much about driving cars. But, God bless him, somehow he got me through the driving test. It was a proud moment when I told Grandma. And nice to settle down to Flash Gordon again.

∽

Some weeks after the test, on a sunny spring day, Grandma told me to go up to Mr Haygarth's garage that afternoon. 'He wants to see you,' was all I could get out of her. I presumed he'd got the new ball bearings for my bike.

I liked Mr Haygarth because his taxi used to take us to Giggleswick station once a year for our summer holiday to Morecambe. He wasn't in the garage when I got there, he was round the back. He didn't see me as I peered around the corner; he was looking sort of vacant and faraway – even sad. Ever so slowly he was polishing the bonnet of his big black taxi. It gleamed. He spotted me and beckoned me over.

'Grandma sent me, Mr Haygarth.'

'I know, lad, her and me's been having a chat. Like the taxi, we're getting older, but with a bit of care there's a mile or two in all of us yet. Look after this old girl,' he said, stroking the bonnet. 'Your grandma always did look right comfy in her'.

He handed me the keys and turned into the shadows of his garage. I didn't say anything. I couldn't believe it. I just got in and moved off as gently as I knew how. She still had that lovely smell of leather that I'd got to know from our annual trip.

Grandma was sitting on the sofa when I

dropped the sneck on our back door. She had on her blue dress, blue coat and the big blue wide hat with fruit on that Mrs Embley had left her when she'd died. It was Sunday Best like you'd never seen. The spitting image of the Queen Mum.

Before I could say a word she said, 'Right, Terry, we'll go down the back street in her, then slowly through Settle, then slowly back through Settle. Then, if we've got enough petrol, we'll go through again.'

We got to the car and I opened the passenger side door for Grandma. 'Thank you,' she said, 'but I'd prefer to sit in the back. It's more dignified.'

Heads peered all over backyard gates all the way down the narrow back street as the Queen Mum rode graciously along. 'I enjoyed that,' she said as we turned the corner. 'Did you see Bessie Turner's face?'

We joined the main road and headed for the market place. She wound the left-hand window down and started the regal waves, real slow and elegant like. 'Stop,' she said, spotting one of her friends loaded down with shopping, 'we'll give her a lift.'

I was enjoying this. Grandma's face was a picture and it brightened up even more as we passed the cricket field. The brass band concert was just finishing and they were doing the National Anthem.

Danny Boy

〰

After two years in prep school I learned that ammo was not just things we threw at each other down the back street. *Amo* also meant I love in Latin. The Barbarians were always having a bust-up with somebody and the Romans seemed definitely pushy. They had, however, invented central heating and indoor swimming pools. Their open sewage system called the Cloaca Maxima, which flowed right through their towns, didn't sound very healthy, though.

Grandad wasn't particularly impressed by this information and suggested that it would only come in useful if I got a job with the council. In the meantime, I was about to move up to the big school where there would be a lot of changes to come to terms with. Tradition abounded. It made you feel safe once you knew what to expect but there was always the first time.

We started at eight in the morning and came home after evening prayers at nine in the evening. On Saturdays we left at five. We had study rooms which took three or four boys, packed in like sardines. There were two rows of adjoining studies and a corridor down the middle. We draped our walls with coloured cloths, anything to make it more homely. By eight-fifteen every morning all the studies had to be ready for inspection. Two prefects – screws, we called them – came around to check that our waste bin, the swogger, was empty. They ran a finger along the ledges and bookshelves hoping for dust, sometimes even bringing their own to catch us out. If they did we got punishment drill – fifteen or thirty minutes of vicious PT held on Tuesdays and Thursdays in the quadrangle so others could watch.

At half past eight the bell tolled for morning assembly in the main hall. Scurrying across the quadrangle like ants, you just hoped you'd grabbed the right books for the first three lessons. Then

through the big oak door into semi-darkness, up the well-worn sandstone steps, past the stained-glass windows and into the vast hall. The masters all assembled at the front in black gowns, some trimmed with ermine, some covered with chalk dust. The Headmaster came in last and we all stood as he made his way to the lectern at the front. Then we had prayers.

❧

It was a bit of a shock to see all the boys in the swimming pool with no cossies on. They reckoned cossies weren't hygienic but I'd get locked up if I tried it in the river. The swimming pool was fed from a spring off the limestone scars above the school. The icy water certainly made everything equal and belly flops were bad news.

Feeling poorly at school wasn't a good idea. Whatever you were suffering from, the sweats would develop as you opened the green door of the sanatorium. There were always quarantine signs on doors, two or three boys in beds looking ghastly, windows flung open and curtains blowing, hot poultices and boils ready for lancing.

We had our own army, complete with guns and everything. They called it the Officer Training Corps or Combined Cadet Force. What it meant was if there was a war, in theory we'd have learned enough stuff and done enough tests to jump the queue and become instant Majors and Generals.

'Maybe that's why we take so long winning wars, with folk like you lot leading,' was Grandad's opinion, while I was bulling my boots. Mind you, he wasn't so keen to have it known that he'd ordered his mortar platoon to fly at a cabbage patch one dark night in Flanders. He was a sergeant up till then.

Monday and Wednesday afternoons were corps days. Everybody was in boots, gaiters and either denims or battledress. We'd have eight platoons marching around the quad, roaming the countryside, doing arms drill or map reading. The armoury was the best place with its lines of rifles in racks, the heavy smell of oil from pull-throughs, and Major Wardle in charge, his chest out and proud as if we were real troups he was leading.

Speech day was the highlight of his year. A mass of parents surrounded the quad waiting for us. But first a final inspection from Major Wardle, as we stood with gleaming buckles and boots, out of sight behind the library. It took weeks to get ready for it.

Our band, dressed in leopardskin robes with tassels, would strike up. Then we followed on in ranks as the Drum Major hurled the silver-headed mace skywards and caught it cleanly in his outstretched white leather glove.

Governors and important people in posh hats clinked sherry glasses on the lawn with the

Headmaster, watching us approach. Bragging boys, who'd left the year before and now puffed on a Senior Service, leaned on their sports cars and introduced their girlfriends.

Oddie's mum made hundreds of cakes for speech day. I thought she was a real hard worker and it was only years later that I found out they owned the biggest bakery in Burnley.

Sport still remained a problem for me. Rugger was the school game and classroom unknowns could become school heroes. My system of tackling was to jump on to folks' backs, cling on and wear them down. It wasn't a technique that was popular with anybody. The list of sports was endless. Apart from rugger there were cricket, boxing, gymnastics, fives, swimming and diving. Grandad even bought me a punch bag for boxing which we put up in our old hut. Even that beat me. When I hit it, it swung back and knocked me out. Everyone got their house colours for some sport, but not me.

Then they tried me on the shooting range and I gawped at the ten bullseyes on my card. I was used to bobbing sparrows so these targets were sitting ducks.

One evening after lessons, a notice went up on the house noticeboard.

House Colours – Shooting – Wilson, T.
R.E.S. Taylor – Housemaster

I kept going up and down past the noticeboard, leaning on it on one elbow, waiting for passers-by to see it. The next day I had my coloured scarf and tried to rub a bit of the newness off it.

Within weeks of a new young housemaster starting we knew we'd got someone special. His hair was smoothed flat to the side. The rest of him looked like a bedraggled vicar. What's more, he was big into bird watching. He was a new breed for a school like ours.

One day he came up with a real surprise. He called us to his study to explain. There were about thirty of us waiting in his study where his ties and shirts were strewn everywhere and the oboe that he struggled with was propped in the corner. He flustered in, dressed in tennis shorts, knees and all.

'What do you think about trying something new in your spare time? It will mean early starts before lessons and late finishes after prayers. And even Saturday nights.' There was a dumb silence. 'How about,' he said, 'early morning sunrise expeditions to the top of one of the local peaks to see the sun rise? Early-morning swims in freezing Stainworth Foss or midnight orienteering expeditions?' Now this sounded definitely us.

'We'll need transport,' he said. Beckoning us over to the outside window, he pointed proudly to his latest acquisition. It was a well-worn, black Rolls-Royce with a silver lady on the front and a long body. In fact it had seen many bodies in its years as a hearse. There was a stampede to sign up as the first volunteers.

Mind you, hearses going through country villages at four in the morning carrying passengers with their faces covered in burned cork aren't everyone's cup of tea, especially policemen's. But the fun we had on those expeditions was worth all the inconveniences that accompanied them.

As sixth formers, our school days ended in the school chapel perched high on a hill top overlooking the school. At a midnight service, lit only by two flickering candles on the altar, 'Danny Boy' drifted gently from the organ as the door closed on our childhoods.

PART THREE

Christmas Goose

૭

W e always had a goose for Christmas. Grandad would do it slowly overnight, at mark two for an hour then down to nought. The grease was drained off twice, put into jars for winter chests, a ritual faithfully followed. When Grandma died, Grandad, Mum and I carried on the tradition. We had some happy Christmases but Grandma's secret mixture for sage and onion stuffing died with her. Despite our best efforts, we couldn't reproduce it.

We'd see Edgar's geese all year on Huntsworth Moor at the top of the dale. Edgar and his brother Harold were at school with Mum which explained why when most people didn't get a goose, we did. Edgar and Harold's place was like

Wuthering Heights, wild and desolate. They were hardly ever seen. Only the farm chimney told they were still on this earth.

One year the goose hadn't come. It always came two days before Christmas so Mum phoned. 'Send the lad up after morning milking,' said Edgar.

It was seven o'clock as my old Cortina clattered up the pot-holed track to the farm. Nothing had changed; the same broken machinery was still rusting in the yard. It took courage to knock on Edgar's door. It creaked open a few inches. Two eyes peered out of the semi-darkness, pink like a ferret's.

'Is it Dorothy's lad? You'll be after a goose?'

'Aye, that's right, Edgar.'

'With thee in a minute.' The door shut again.

When it opened again I could see the kitchen table and it was bare. This seemed a bit odd. Edgar's geese were always plucked to perfection and wrapped in greaseproof paper with the weight and price scribbled on in purple pencil, the sort you lick the end of to make it work.

'Come on then,' said Edgar pulling on his wellies, 'get that sack.' It was a break from normal practice but he wasn't a man to argue with. 'No time this year, too damned busy,' muttered Edgar as he slipped open the field gate. 'Right, which do you want?' he said, scanning the hillside. Good grief, they were still on the hoof! 'Get up there and fetch them down and I'll grab it.' Things were not going to plan here – well, not my plan. But I either rounded up my own goose or settled for a Christmas dinner of roast potatoes, apple sauce, stuffing and corned beef! So up the field I ventured.

They're nasty things are geese when they don't know you, and they've got this in-built time-clock near Christmas. But down they went – well, some of them. The rest went over the wall and along Fellings Road at a fair rate of knots. 'They'll be back,' screamed Edgar as I wondered which lot to go after.

'That goose'll do, Edgar,' I said pointing to the nearest and pulling a cowclap off my left shoe. He had it straight into the sack and tied with a piece of bailing twine from his jacket pocket. 'I reckon it's about a twelve pounder,' said Edgar raising the sack from the ground. 'I'll settle for four pound ten shillings. You'll be all right – plucking is easy.'

൜

'That you, lad? called Grandad, as I dropped the sack at the back door.

'Aye, it's me, Grandad.' He was pretty deaf so this would take some explaining.

'Got goose all right?'

'Sort of, Grandad.'

'Well, just put it on the draining board.'

'Think it'll fall off, Grandad.'

'Put it on a plate then.'

'Don't think that'll help, Grandad. Damn!' It slipped and the string came off the sack. 'It's coming through, Grandad.'

'What the ... it's still alive!'

'Edgar couldn't do it, Grandad, too busy.'

'It has to go into t'oven today, lad.'

'It'll need some help, Grandad. I'll go get the yard brush.'

'Has it done something?'

'No, but it will shortly. Oh heck, it's around the back of the sofa – budgie's over. Get it into the kitchen, Grandad. Eh up, it's off upstairs. Gotcha. Into the kitchen with you. Right, I'll lay it on the floor while you get that brush shaft across its neck. Put your feet on each end of the shaft. Ready? Hold fast and I'll tug.'

'Is it dead yet, lad?'

'It's winking a lot, Grandad. Doesn't like it. Oops, it's flapping again – keep still!'

'Who, me or t'goose?'

'We'd better make sure, Grandad. Hang on, I'll get something.'

'You're not going to ...'

'What else?'

Just as the axe fell, Mum's curlers and nightie-clad shoulders peered round the bottom of the stairs. She woke the neighbours with her screams.

It was the quietest Christmas dinner we'd ever had. And there was lots left.

Hunter's Last Night

〜

My mind wandered. I was alone. The light from old Bill Limmer's cottage was barely visible. It came and went with each heavy flurry of snow. My flesh tightened with the cold, my movements slowed. I could hardly see anything, not even the river a few feet away. Two more ducks had come in with an unseen glide and a splash. They'd known I was there so they'd waited till now. I switched the torch on and wing beats from the river melted up into the falling snow.

I turned the light to my feet. Red blood dripped in sticky lumps from the mallard I'd shot earlier. Its colours outshone the torch. Maybe I'd fall into a ditch when I walked back

to old Bill's; that would sort of make things more equal.

Maybe it was time to stop. For years we'd enjoyed the wind, the frost, the snow. With icy eyebrows, straining eyes and ears, a wild challenge was shared. Was it now time to part? To let the gun rust? I though of Peter Scott who'd shot on the Norfolk Fens. Our instincts had changed in the same way. Rather than shooting the duck and geese, we had both fallen in love with the sheer beauty of being in their company, sharing their elements.

My tears froze. I walked away from the driftwood hide, confused. Barbed wire sunk into my knee. I felt warmer already.

Uncle Teddy

꙳

Uncle Teddy did magic lantern shows for kids' parties and entertained the old folks at afternoon teas, providing ginger snaps and a warm welcome. He was everybody's uncle Teddy. At the village fete, he was always in his van, E. CROWTHER – PLUMBER painted on the side and a black and white dog sitting on the bonnet. His Master's Voice loudspeaker on top defied the rain with 'Land of Hope and Glory', challenged only by a bellowing compère from the Women's Institute introducing the next event.

I needed an old fire grate. Ours had burned through after lasting years. Uncle Teddy's shop was down a ginnel off the main street. His sign hung precariously. 'It'll drop off one day,' he'd say, quite unconcerned.

'I got six fire grates that size in '53,' said Teddy, when I asked. The calendar on the wall behind him said 1979. 'They'll be in the back.' I felt reassured as he led me through his Aladdin's cave. Clouds of dust rose with our footsteps as we passed a few Potterton boilers and a few 'Don't know what those are'. Then his face gleamed; his Olympiad torch was raised in one hand and a fire grate in the other. I smiled and nodded.

Teddy looked glum. 'That's the easy bit,' he said, clambering back. 'Now let's get to the office.'

He pointed to stacks of papers around the sides of the room. 'Right, now all the bills and receipts are there somewhere. I started here in '29 and they're all in piles by the year, though some might be mixed up.'

'Got it,' he shrieked with delight after only an hour. He'd found them in the '61s. 'And I never paid for them,' said Teddy, 'I'd better chase that up.' The bill said two pounds, thirteen shillings and sixpence for six. 'I knew I'd got six,' he muttered with satisfaction. 'A good memory never fades. It's just remembering where you've put them. How much is that?' he wondered hand on chin, cursing the decimal converter that he'd bought before D Day. 'Tell you what, we'll call it half-a-crown. It was Coronation year when I bought them so we'll split the difference!'

∽

One of Teddy's tales I'll never forget. It was a Saturday night, about half past eight, when his phone rang. He and his wife were dressed up for their weekly night out. It was the man you couldn't argue with, Dr Donald. Whatever the ailment Dr Donald's treatment would be more or less the same, whether it was mumps or warts.

'The sink's blocked, Teddy. She's in a right state. Overflow's failing, drips everywhere – it's an emergency.' Teddy smiled. 'Be there in ten minutes,' he said and went for his toolkit. His van shot up Dr Donald's drive, chippings flying everywhere. There were lights on in each room and a party was in full swing. The housekeeper opened the door. Teddy was ushered with his toolkit through to the kitchen where water was swilling all over.

Dr Donald entered. 'Thank heavens you've come. What do you think?' Teddy peered closely at the dripping suds, leaned over the sink and tapped it three times with two fingers. He straightened up, looked at the doctor, shook his head and muttered, 'She's in a bad way.' Then he reached into his toolkit, threw in two Alka Seltzers and said, 'But she'll be all right in the morning!' There was a distant belch from the plug-hole and the blockage was freed.

Gate Holes

෴

It was the Monday before Christmas. Jack and I had gone over to his brother's on his old motorbike. It must have been about half past nine, on a wild night, as we were on our way back. We were meandering about a bit because we couldn't see much through our goggles. Sleet and snow were blowing rotten off the moor tops and through the gate holes.

I could just make out the car, parked up at the end of the lane near the Gamecock Pub. On went the flashing blue light. They'll never believe us, I thought, as they pulled us in. They'll not know Jack's brother's a butcher.

The old bike slithered to a halt, nearly into the ditch. 'Silly sods. Nowt else better to do,' said Jack.

'Evening, gentlemen,' said the policeman, getting out of the Granada. 'Wobbling a bit, aren't we, sir?'

'Stop sticking your face up to mine,' said Jack. 'And you'd wobble in this wind. Haven't got wipers on me goggles – not like thee.'

'You wouldn't have had a drink, would you, sir?'

'No, and we're not likely to, stuck here chatting with thee!'

Then the policeman said it. I knew he would, it's always the same where we live, we have it every Christmas – the turkey check. 'Some thieving going on, sir. We're having to check vehicles. Turkeys being stolen. Expect you've got some, eh?'

I winced. We'd never get home for a pint. 'Turkeys,' said Jack, 'well, there's one in each pannier.'

'On your way, sir. And drive slowly.'

Funny how you can sweat in winter. It would have been all right if the wind hadn't gusted through the gate hole as we set off. The top of one of the panniers blew up. There were feathers everywhere.

They don't half start quick, them Granadas!

To Top it Off

∽

That third prize with the cauli had started something. First it got me mad but then it showed what could be done if you knew the ropes. And maybe this idea that all you need for successful gardening is green fingers is rubbish after all.

There were plenty of books about gardening but little about growing veg to win prizes. Apparently the varieties aren't important. Top exhibitors even breed their own super strains. The seeds in the shop weren't much good, not for this game. It seemed there was no one man, either, who had all the answers. There was a top man for each veg somewhere in Britain and I went to every length to find their names. I'd see

an article in the paper by someone and I did my best to track him down. My bedroom became the operation room, complete with a map with flags in and names and addresses.

Eventually, painstakingly, my collection of information grew and within three years the local show benches were littered with my first-prize cards. I learned many tricks too. Carrot were grown in bore holes three foot deep and filled in with the fine soil from mole heaps. Potatoes were grown in peat so there was not a mark on them and they came out shiny as pearls. Runner beans, when picked, were splinted to a stick and wrapped in a wet cloth overnight. They'd be as straight as gun barrels the next day. Peas were grown just one or two to a plant and beetroot was fed with road salt so the flesh was nice and dark.

I'd seen some of the dodges as well. A little milk or Vaseline made potatoes sparkle. Wires inside flower stems made them straight. Worst of all, the exhibitor's emergency kit; things like using nail varnish to stick a replacement flower on the stem of a gladiolus. It would last through judging, get a prize, even Best Exhibit, then fall off by the time the show opened.

Then there was the coarse art of showmanship. The exhibitor who'd go along the benches as you were laying out your veg, muttering very loudly, 'It's a pity there's a mark on the back of one of your lovely potatoes,' hoping the judge, ready for starting, would be in earshot. What a game it all was!

The other problem is that if one person keeps winning year after year, it spoils the show for everybody. So I entered local shows less and less. What I needed was a high to go out on. Something not local but which even local folk could be proud of.

᪥

The chance came. A national competition was to be held the following year at that mecca of meccas, Southport Show. It was the longest runner bean contest, organised by a national gardening magazine. This offered a real challenge because I knew of no bean capable of enormous lengths. Eventually I found a retired breeder who'd worked at Kew Gardens. We wrote to each other. He had a few seeds and wanted to keep the strain going. I promised to give it my best and six seeds popped through the letter box.

I needed the help of my friend Ray for this. He'd retired from the army and now ran the school cadet force. It called for a military operation and his big greenhouse. The seeds went in on the first of April. Within days the shoots were coming through and growing by the minute. 'Sure they're not rhubarb?' chuckled Ray as gigantic leaves began to develop. Then came the flower stems. Instead of the normal few inches they were two to three feet long.

The next problem was how to pollinate the flowers. And this is where army training pays off. You learn initiative.

Ray organised bee hunts. A few boys from the school, volunteered by Ray, were issued with jam jars. There were many such hunts but most of the bees got back out of the greenhouse and the rest usually got up Ray's trousers. We needed a less vicious sort of beasty.

'Moths don't sting,' said Ray, 'and electric light attracts them.' We tried it. We rigged up a 60-watt bulb in the middle of the greenhouse and came back after dark. There were plenty of moths around the light bulb but none near the plants. The next morning I went into the paper shop. 'What's you and your mad mate up to?' asked the newsagent. 'Nothing special,' I muttered, feeling a bit down. 'Well what's he buying six sets of Christmas tree lights for in April?' came the reply. 'Brilliant!' I shouted and shot out of the door.

That night the greenhouse looked spectacular. Twinkling lights twisted around each runner bean stem and moths were going crazy on the flowers. It all went to plan and the beans set on the plants.

By high summer it was a steaming jungle inside the greenhouse with plants growing up and away through the corrugated plastic roof, coming out like monster ivy and trailing down the outside with the glimpse of a gigantic bean here and there in the undergrowth. Panes of glass collapsed under the strain. It was impossible to get inside the building so we had to use an old stirrup pump to spray feed and water through the open door. 'We'll need a machete when it's time,' said Ray.

With two days to the show, in full protective clothing, we clawed our way into the jungle. The best bean was over two feet long and we knew we had a chance.

The bean had to be sent to Southport, where they laid out all the entries. We made it a special box, lined it with cotton wool, placed the bean inside and took it to the Post Office.

'First or second?' chuntered the man looking up from behind the counter.

'Second's no good,' we said, 'and neither's third or fourth.' So off it went first class.

The day of the show, we went straight to the runner bean tent. There were lines of beans all along the benches. Lots of jostling. But ours wasn't there. It was on its own table – next to the cup.

Money Spinners

∽

Some of the little money-spinning ventures I embarked on proved quite costly.

Mushroom growing, according to the advert, was guaranteed. The kit arrived, complete with mine and Ray's names on as being Registered Suppliers to Covent Garden. But it didn't mention how to extinguish a mountain of fermenting straw that had reached ignition point, or that Ray would end up without a hut.

Guppie breeding in fish tanks got off to a good start until the November power cuts. Our other sideline of terrapins to be turned into souvenir ashtrays of Giggleswick was doomed before it got off the ground.

However, this one had the distinct scent of

success as we came up the track to Holly Dean Farm. The sign said it all: FERRETS FOR SALE.

There was nobody about, just a couple of collies on chains barking their heads off; but strung out on a line, there must have been fifty or so rabbits. We winked at each other as out from the shippon came the farmer.

'I've only two young 'uns left,' he said. 'There's been a run on ferrets what with the hills being wick with rabbits. But these young 'uns are catching on and I'll let you have George too. He'll show 'em the ropes.'

'Do they bite?' I asked.

'Not if you treat 'em right from young. Play with them and handle them a lot, then you'll be okay. Mind you, George is a different matter,' he warned.

'Who's George? asked Ray.

'An old dog ferret,' was the reply. 'He can shift rabbits but mind you always lift him by the back of the neck. He'll not nip you then.'

Round the back of the shippon we came to two white bundles frolicking about in a pen made from chicken wire. He lifted the top and handed

me and Ray one apiece. They scrambled everywhere, up our jackets, round our necks and all
over the place. 'They're good are these,' I said,
getting more enthusiastic about our plan by the
minute.

'Aye. Now here's George,' he said, sliding back
the black bolt on a very sturdy wooden box. The
box started shaking. Out popped George's head,
blood dripping from a full set of razor teeth. 'It's
just the rabbit liver,' muttered the farmer as I
moved sharply back two paces. 'His reward for
them rabbits he got this morning.' Clearly George
would have to be Ray's personal ferret.

In the next few weeks, our new business inno-
vation bit the dust. One of the little ferrets was
last seen on the middle shelf between the
Babychams and Britvics in our local. The other
one became redundant as myxomatosis struck
the local rabbit population. And George cost us a
bill from Mr Harger, the local vet.

One day George turned really nasty so I took
him to Mr Harger. He picked George up and
turned him upside down. 'This'll soon calm him
down,' he said, picking up a scalpel. Castration

seemed a bit extreme, even though George's behavior did call for severe restraint. So when the vet sliced open the tick that had been driving him crazy, I think I was more relieved than George was.

The Quarry

༄

The sign said NO UNAUTHORISED ENTRY. What's more, the bottom part was surrounded by pine trees so you couldn't see a lot. But most days, about three o'clock, you could hear the big bangs from the quarry. Very gradually the quarry nibbled into the limestone scar.

A narrow path wound up the steep hillside, past the firs and on to the open top. Up there amongst the bracken, rabbits lived and grouse sheltered in the winter. As a lad, it was a place where I'd taken my sandwiches and a bottle of Tizer. The quarry was surrounded by a rickety old fence so that you couldn't fall over.

I'd sit by that fence and watch the kestrel soar on the updraft, then hang motionless, seeming to look down on me, surrounded by wild pansies and thyme. Lying back in the bracken listening to the sound of skylarks I could go undetected by the hare as he bobbed past.

Each limestone rock held a fossil. Cockle shells, stems of anemonies and snail shapes; layer after layer of them like a history book on its side. How could all this have been under water way up here?

Shutters of crows squawked out from the quarry sides. The men, way down below in the bottom, their hammers swinging into the piles of limestone, occasionally stopped to wipe the sweat from their bodies. Breaking and filling, they called it. Each man had to fill his truck and then heave it back down his own metal track to the kilns. Then an overhead railway took the buckets of lime, weaving into the distance towards the station.

Grandad told me stories about men he'd known who'd been hurt in this job; how black powder could go wrong and how men had to dangle over the edge on chains or ropes. The men in the quarry worked hard for their living but there was little else for them in the way of work round here. The fence hardly ever moved back so the path was safe.

I knew all the shades of green under the edge of the scar, the colours of autumn and the green haze of spring. Here was the top of my world and a view that spelled peace. Lines of sheep filed by on the footpath, passing the cairn which had

been built up over the years by schoolboys, walkers, lovers, people with memories.

But as boy grew into man, metal monsters moved in. A nibble was no longer enough. They ripped up her spine with their fossil-fuelled machines. Now the path has gone.

D Day

～

Planning for D Day fell between Bookkeeping for Farmers and Profitable Pickling. Grandad reckoned I was in good company and it was my own daft fault for getting involved in the first place.

The Royal Mint had run a special course for me and a few others. Registered Trainers were the only people in the country licensed to possess the new decimal coinage six months before D Day. I trained people at Johnson and Johnson, where I worked, so I was also kitted up with a picture flipboard of the new coins, a nice little board with felt-tip pens, a pack of snap playing cards with pictures of old and new coins, a bag of future money and a suitcase to keep it all in.

The word got around. The local Chamber of Trade was starting to get the breeze up on discovering there was no way they could avoid D Day, so they got on to Norris Lockley, who organised the night classes at the high school.

'Can you help me out?' Norris asked. I agreed and a few days later when I passed Lambert's newsagents, the weekly paper was out and there on the billboard it said:

National

Company Executive

To train Local Traders in

Decimalisation

I shot inside for a night class brochure and there was D Day Training sandwiched between tight-fisted farmers and pickles.

Local speculation was rife. Who was this mysterious high-powered character? No name had been given. Neither did the brochure say that the training I'd done at work had been mainly concerned with the price changes of sausage rolls, bacon butties and toasted teacakes for the benefit of the canteen ladies. It had gone quite well, apart from a hiccup over the sarnies, and Bessie not getting into the spirit of role playing in the canteen after work. 'Cos we don't do pies on Mondays,' she insisted. And the Executive bit in the brochure only applied to the use of the loo at my firm, which had separate ones for executives and workers.

∽

I knew I'd got the night right. Parked outside the high school was a flock of tractors, the Mercs being safely locked up at home, away from the tax man. Old ladies were staggering in with baskets of chutney jars. The doorman, seeing my sweat and the size of my bulging suitcase, must have decided I was a farmer and directed me to Room 2.

I smelled the Bookkeeping for Farmers as I passed, and the chatter of clinking jam jars identified the picklers. I turned a corner and the sign on the door, D DAY, identified where I belonged. There was a roomful of noisy 60-year-old kids sitting two to a desk. Someone shuffled up to make room for me and the din continued.

I put down my case by the blackboard. There was a sudden deathly silence, broken only by Alice Eglin from Corsets and Foundations.

'It's nobbut Dorothy Hird's lad,' she announced at the top of her voice. The room sounded like a deflating tyre and faces started to relax.

According to my instruction kit, a good start was to explain the obvious advantages of decimalisation. Somebody asked what this had to do with pickles, then headed off for the other room. Alice, clearly taking command, reckoned they were already in one and that Teddy Percy from plumbing should put his filthy pipe out in class.

'We've problems enough with new ideas,' chuntered Alice, 'and it'll never catch on. Just look at this.'

She unzipped a bag and brought out two fine examples of Cross Your Heart and Little X. 'They don't beat whalebone. Now price 'em up, Terry, there's a love.'

I thought it best to switch to the recommended technique of 'Let's pretend we're all going to Alice's shop.' The men refused to play. Then Alice got quite personal with her 'Where do you find it tends to rub, dear?' complete with the Les Dawson bosom shuffle. That got the men giggling, so we turned to plumbing examples instead. Alice declared that she'd had Teddy once and never again. Teddy muttered something about ballcocks.

The special snap playing cards worked all right until the cheating started and two farmers popped in to ask if we'd got a card school going and could they swap classes.

The instruction kit said, 'End the first session on a confident note,' so I resorted to the conversion tables. They were happier once they could compare new prices with real money and it would mean no price increases, what with trade being the way it was.

I passed Alice's shop on D Day. She'd got everything dual priced and you could pay either way. However, if you paid in decimal you got it for half price. Well, that's what her sign said.

Where the Heart Is

⌇

The trouble with country doctors is that they really bother about you. Ours had just retired and the new one was a lady. She started with my sore throat, moving on to how Grandad and Mum were keeping, then on to the inevitable. 'Any girl-friends yet?'

'No,' I replied.

'Still not, eh! And you'll be what now?'

Then came the mixed questions between 'Any problems?' and 'How did you find Public School?'

One summer it all changed. It was a night like any other in our village pub, except there were two strangers at the bar, and women at that. One had a strong resemblance to Dame Edna Everage while the other wore a smart candy-striped jacket and was quieter. They both had their hair done the same way in an almighty wave to the side like an Aussie army hat. Dame Edna, or Shirley as it transpired, soon had a devoted audience as she recounted tales of Australia in a slow drawl.

I got chatting with the quieter one. Apparently their family used to own one of the local pubs but had left for Australia twenty-five years previously, for the sake of their mother's health. After all that time, Marion and her sister were back on holiday.

Our conversation inevitably turned to the Dales. Marion told me how much she missed them and she still treasured memories of George the gamekeeper, the hot-pot suppers they'd made at their pub and the story of the Food Inspector. During the war their dad kept half a pig hidden under the log pile. When a government food inspector turned up and said he would be staying with them while he checked all the pubs in the area, her mum had asked him straight, 'Are you going to have a look round here or do you want to eat right at breakfast?'

He chose to enjoy his breakfast and concentrated on checking the other pubs.

Marion and I made arrangements to meet the next day and have a drive round the countryside that she missed so much. I pulled up the car at their old pub and walked round the boarded-up windows. There was a glimpse of the scullery and the old table where she'd plucked grouse, the rusted Aga range and her mum's first fridge, now spray-painted with graffiti. The pigsty had fallen. But the sound of memories was still strong.

We climbed up to the moors, through unfurling bracken and the smell of thyme, up on to the limestone scars. Beneath was the valley which she'd seen only in dreams for the last twenty-five years. She used to wake up crying. It had been her mum's favourite place, as it was hers, as it was mine.

All afternoon we sat and looked down the valley, saying little and seeing nobody. The landscape had not changed at all in the years she'd been away.

My mum was surprised to find me spending so much time in the company of this older woman, but was happier when she learned that Marion's parents had been her old mates from The Golden Lion. Then there were endless tales of the old days between them. Too soon Marion's holiday drew to a close.

᠉

Two years later I was still having problems with the doctor's probing questions, but now there was a difference. At Heathrow I awaited the arrival of a Qantas flight. She was coming back to our Scars.

We both said, 'I do.' The registrar put down her glasses, then turned from us to Mum and said, 'And what do you think, Dorothy?'

A Passing Mention

⌇

'You don't write much about me in your stories,' muttered Mum.

'I do,' I said. 'You get a passing mention.'

'Your carrots are passing mentions,' she said. 'Tramps get pages.'

'They're important,' I said. 'They're ... past tense. You're ... present tense. I prefer you that way.'

'Glad you've noticed,' she said. 'What do you want for supper?'

⌇

It was the run-up to Christmas. I'd upped the housekeeping money so Mum could get extra goodies in. Mr Kipling's mince pies, vol-au-vents, and Icelandic prawns for the freezer. Bits and bobs she sidled away, including her whisky.

The doctors were doing a brisk winter trade, Mum helping with her regular winter bronchitis and steady forty-a-day filter-tipped, half hidden in the knitting bag.

Nightly Christmas turkey bingo sessions had started. The Catholic Hall on Monday. Tuesday the Settle Social Club. Wednesday the Langcliffe Village Institute and the rugby club to end the week.

What with her crackly chest, wonky legs and blood pressure, Mum had taken to travelling everywhere by taxi, regularly explaining to the driver that he was – sexually explicit – late again. If he'd didn't pull his finger out she'd not get her usual bingo seat. And he should have stuck to being a farmer anyway.

❧

That Saturday night her chest seemed to be getting the better of her, and she went to bed early. She couldn't settle with the breathing and every hour popped downstairs. We chatted, then she was off up again.

About half past ten she missed the last few steps on the way down, crashing her face and ribs against the wall. The doctor came. No broken bones; a gashed face that needed stitching, but she'd settle for 'butterfly closures' – she was scared stiff at the thought of hospital, 'Cos they don't come out at my age.' Her ribs were badly bruised, but she could stay at home if we looked after her night and day. We nodded and she gripped Marion's hand tightly.

Mum looked like she'd done ten rounds with Frank Bruno, what with the rapidly blackening face and closing eyes. She struggled the next few days, straining to breathe, trying to get comfy. We checked on her regularly, finding that she'd discovered yet another 'odd drop of whisky' in her bedroom.

Christmas Eve, Marion put the goose into the oven to cook slowly overnight. We sat quietly. Then came the shuffling noise: Mum was on her way down to check on the goose. Satisfied with that, she wanted to play 'half an hour of cards'. Through swollen eyes and aching ribs, she laughed at beating us. Then her eyes twinkled, as best they could.

'I want to see the world before I go,' she said, sort of prophetically.

I quivered. 'Complicated, Mum,' I said. 'It'll take a bit of fixing and pretty expensive.'

'It isn't,' she insisted. 'Seventeen quid, from Lambert's shop in Settle – 'course there was another three quid for Edith next door to get it back in the taxi. It's under the stairs,' she said. 'I've always wanted one.' Opened up, the large cardboard box revealed a two-foot-across globe of the world. Mostly blue.

'One last hand of cards,' she said, sitting there, smiling, with the world at her feet. 'Then we'll pack up.'

'She's won,' said Marion, totalling the scores.

'She has,' I said. 'Definitely, she has.'

ง

Determined to do things right, Mum was properly dressed on Christmas morning, ready for present-opening. We sat around the crackling log fire, the mist rolling down the fells outside.

'Couldn't wrap 'em,' she said. 'Got George the gamekeeper to make 'em for you.'

She handed one to Marion and one to me.

'Brilliant, Mum,' I said, marvelling at the carving on the hazel walking stick.

'Aye,' she replied, her face clearly pleased. 'But think on, take care of 'em. Sticks like that don't grow on trees.'

Mum settled down for 'Just a bit of Christmas dinner, to say I've had some', then was happy to go for a lie down in bed.

Early evening, she asked if we'd tuck her in so

she could try and settle down for the night. Marion and I sat downstairs, talking quietly. We checked on her regularly during the evening. Marion went in again at half past ten, but after only a minute or two she was back in the room. She looked at me and said gently, 'I think she's gone, love.'

Dr Bill came. We sat talking about Mum and how often she had made him laugh. Bill said he'd sign the certificate in the morning.

The bedroom walls told Mum's story. Drawing-pinned memories of holidays. I opened the music box. It played her favourite tune, *'Una Paloma Blanca'* – the white dove of freedom. Then quietly I closed the door.

'We'll need Tom Seggar as undertaker, and a burial in the churchyard,' I said to Marion. 'No one else will do, what with Mum always having laid folk out for him.'

Dawn broke on Boxing Day, a Thursday. Morning phone calls to Tom's house brought no answer. Then came the news, 'He's away for Christmas.'

'How long?' No one knew. And the Registrar's

Office had a notice on the door. CLOSED FOR CHRISTMAS – OPEN MONDAY. Five days away. All we had was a death certificate and Mum, upstairs. At least it was official. Marion had done the laying out, as she'd once been a nurse. Dr Bill popped in daily to see if we'd found Tom yet.

Mum's bedroom window got to being fully open. The central heating was off and my thoughts were moving to pushing up the Icelandic prawns and scampi in the freezer.

News from the vicarage wasn't helping. The churchyard was full, and we were sort of 'in between' vicars.

'She'd not like a cremation,' I said to Marion in desperation. 'But maybe an urn in Grandma and Grandad's grave might have to do?'

~

The doorbell rang. There stood the highly respected, eighty-odd-year-old undertaker Tom Seggar.

Within minutes he and I were inside the church, Tom poring through the burial records.

The word 'full' had not been entered into the book when Grandad had died some years back.

'Room for doubt,' said Tom to the verger, 'we'll just check.'

Back outside by the watering cans, Tom searched around until he found what he wanted.

'Here,' he said, handing me a twelve-foot-long iron bar. 'Take hold of this. Now, where's Grandma and Grandad's grave?'

I shuddered as we walked on. Then, finally, we got to it.

'Stand right across it,' he told me. 'Ram the rod down as far as it'll go.'

I wondered what six years would have done to Grandad. Feeling for Grandad was taking on a new meaning.

At two foot down the rod stopped solidly. 'Another spot,' urged Tom.

Same again, as the bar and I came to a bone-shaken halt.

'Rocky,' said Tom. 'A last go, wiggle it about a bit.'

I dropped to my knees as the rod sunk down deeply.

'We're okay,' nodded Tom to the verger as we passed the door of the church. 'I'll have the grave digger in this afternoon.'

I headed off for home.

'We've got a problem,' said Marion as I came in through the front door. 'Mum says she wants stew and dumplings.'

'She can't,' I said, 'she's dead.'

'It's in a note,' said Marion, 'I've found it in her drawer. She wants a "do" after the funeral. Mary from the Settle Down Café to make the dumplings and us to book the Concert Room in the Social Club.'

'I've got deeper problems of my own,' I juddered, grabbing a torch and heading off into the twilight.

The planks took some shifting, but the torchlight showed progress, with the pick and shovel having been left in there for the night. And there was no sign of Grandad.

෴

The morning the coffin was lowered a white bird rose high from the churchyard, circling upward, joining the others in effortless motion.

Two weeks later, snowdrops covered the grave.

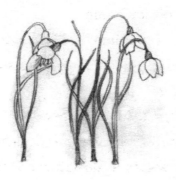

About the Author

～

Terry Wilson was born in Settle, North Yorkshire, in 1945. He started writing at nine years old when he won a Bournville chocolate competition about a cocoa bean; but it has been the Yorkshire Dales and its people that have provided most of his material. He has been previously published in the *Dalesman* magazine and the *Yorkshire Post*.